WEST SUSS[ ]
LITERARY
TRAIL

"exploring, village by village, our rich literary heritage"

PETER ANDERSON &
KEITH MCKENNA

Whilst the authors have walked and researched the entire route for the purposes of this guide, no responsibility can be accepted for any unforeseen circumstances encountered while following it.

The publishers would, however, greatly appreciate any information regarding material changes, and any problems encountered.

Detailed and up-to-date information about the facilities on the route is available on the Trail website www.westsussexliterarytrail.co.uk.

Please go to the 'facilities' page and enter
'Username': WSLT and 'Password': INFO; both uppercase.

The right of Peter Anderson and Keith McKenna to be identified as the authors of this work is hereby asserted pursuant to the Copyright, Design and Patents Act 1988. © Peter Anderson and Keith McKenna.

ISBN 978-0-9549654-3-3

Designed by *IntegrityDesignandPrint@hotmail.co.uk*

Printed by Hastings Printing Company Limited

All photographs © Keith McKenna except where stated.
Front cover: The Blue Idol, Oldhouse Lane, Coolham.
Rear cover: Shelley Fountain, Horsham and St. Richard's Statue, Chichester

First published in 2007 by Per-Rambulations

Larkshill,
Cranston Road,
East Grinstead,
West Sussex,
RH19 3HL.

Tel: 01342 315786
www.Per-Rambulations.co.uk

Contents

Maps

HISTORY

In 2001 West Sussex hosted the South East of England Walking Festival and invited Footprints to take part in the administration. The first half of the Festival was based in Horsham and the second in Chichester but even a cursory glance at the map showed that the idea of moving the event symbolically by walking from one location to the other was not possible. That would take at least four days.

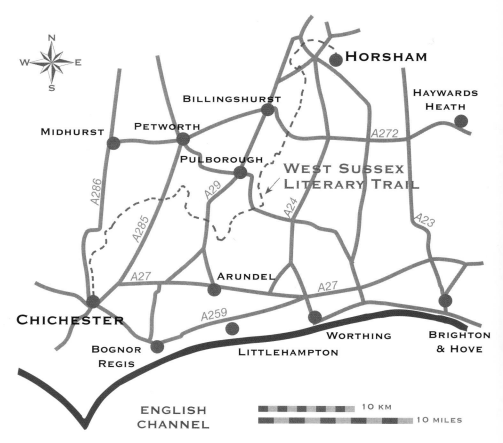

The idea would not go away. A chance meeting between the authors brought a new perspective and a joint venture: a delightful walking Trail with a host of literary associations, that would add interest for the walker and might encourage others to walk.

That is the history but the future is the Trail stretching ahead…

PREFACE

Just now passing out of living memory is the world before the motor car came into general use at a time when the carriage and the horse were the main means of local transport, where people still travelled considerable distances on foot for their daily work and where for longer distances the railway on land and the ship by sea were the transport mode of necessity.

Now many of us walk for pleasure but reading the landscape by its traditional features and the knowledge of the people who lived in the Weald and the Downs is an essential part of enjoying this part of Sussex. In our present times it is the writers and poets who speak to us from the past of things that relate to Sussex of the present.

This Trail is of John Baker and William Cobbett, of Belloc, Blunt and Shelley, of D H Lawrence, Edward Lear and Mervin Peake; the love of the Downs and the Weald is brought to life here along with good men and highway men, saints and smugglers all interwoven with myth, mystery, legend and hard fact which should amply reward the wayfaring reader of these pages.

The Earl of Lytton

GETTING THERE

It was a dull, foggy day when Sherlock Holmes and Dr Watson caught that *"excellent"* two o'clock train from Victoria station en route to Lamberley, south of Horsham, on the trail of the Sussex Vampire.

It may be pure coincidence that their destination was Lamberley and the Trail passes through the village of Amberley that lies to the south west of Horsham.

Although Conan Doyle is more associated with East Sussex he did also know the countryside southwards of Horsham. In 1893 his sister, Connie, married E(rnest) W(illiam) Hornung, the novelist and creator of Raffles, the gentleman burglar, and, for a while, the couple lived at West Grinstead Park on the south side of the road that is now the A272 approximately five miles to the east of where the Trail crosses that road. Towards the end of her life, Conan Doyle's mother took a house almost opposite that she named 'Bowshots Cottage'. A timber framed house called 'Bowshots' stands today on the north side of the A272 at West Grinstead.

Was it here through the marriage that Conan Doyle (and Sherlock Holmes) became acquainted with the hinterland of Sussex? Conan Doyle's own move away from London was yet to come: first to Hindhead in Surrey in 1897 and then into Sussex itself at Crowborough in 1907 .

The aim of the West Sussex Literary Trail is not, however, to hunt Sussex Vampires: nor is there a strong underlying moral purpose to educate or to indulge in a deep exercise of literary criticism. Although there is always the hope that those who encounter the Trail will be tempted to read, and enquire, and walk further, the primary objective is to entertain as a walk and as an introduction to and celebration of the wide diversity of the countryside and literature of West Sussex and some of those who or whose writings are in some way connected with it.

To understand West Sussex the best way is to travel on foot north/south, as the Trails does, cutting across the geological bands running east/west that go to make the county up rather like an immense layer cake lying on its side with some

additions like pieces of fruit in between. Horsham, where the Trail starts, lies at the edge of both the High and the Low Wealds although the route of the Trail passes only through the Low Weald. It crosses the Wealden Greensand, meets the Arun Valley and the Amberley Wild Brooks. It then runs beneath the escarpment of the South Downs before crossing the Downs and descending into the coastal plain and journey's end at Chichester. It is in the main a quiet route across West Sussex and it might be thought that little has happened along the way across the centuries but there are nevertheless important national and international connections.

The geology creates the individual landscape characters of the areas through which the Trail passes: not only the natural features but also what man has made. Before the coming of easier and cheaper forms of transport with the canals and railways local materials were used except for the most prestigious of buildings, particularly in Sussex where the difficulties of transport were notorious. This is reflected along the Trail, the timber framed buildings of the Weald, the local sandstone of the greensand around Nutbourne, flint on the Downs, and the mixed architecture of the coastal plain where the sea eased the import of building materials.

To create a literary trail is a somewhat daunting task. Although 'literary' and 'trail' are interdependent it was essential to develop a walk of beauty that is capable of standing on its own that will be followed irrespective of its literary or any other connections. The literary content holds different perils: especially who should be mentioned. It might be felt that some writers are not sufficiently literary to be included.

The 9th edition of *The Chambers Dictionary* includes "*relating to…literature or the writing of books*" in its definition of 'literary'. The same dictionary, in its definition of 'literature', includes, "*the art of composition in prose and verse, the whole body of literary composition universally…*" Like Molière's

Bourgeois Gentilhomme, who was surprised to discover that he spoke in prose, the authors have unexpectedly found that they contribute to literature: but it does demonstrate that the choice is as wide as the authors care to make it

West Street, Horsham prior to 1964

in pursuit of their primary objective mentioned above. And, maybe, something more will have been achieved if enquiry and discussion have been provoked.

With such a wide base of selection, it would not be possible to include every writer who was born in, came to, went from, wrote about or merely passed through Sussex. Preference, but not altogether, has been given to those who are met along the Trail, have an association with something that can be seen from it, or may be encountered within a narrowish but flexible band on either side of it. Even in these confines some may have been omitted or forgotten. That may too serve to induce further reaction. And one has to stop somewhere in a work of this size but, perhaps, one day, a companion anthology may be created although that will fall to other hands.

There is nothing strange in combining literature and walking. In the late 18th century and the birth of the Romantic movement, walking became more than a mere means of progression for those who could not ride on or behind a horse or be carried. The major English Romantic poets, Wordsworth (1770-1850), Coleridge (1772-1834), Shelley (1792-1822) and Keats (1795-1821) were no strangers to walking.

It is a pity that it has not been possible to uncover a Wordsworthian connection with West Sussex for he was the paradigm of literary walking. In her history of walking, *Wanderlust* (2001), Rebecca Solnit entitles one of her chapters *The Legs of William Wordsworth.* She quotes Thomas

De Quincey, a fellow poet in those days of breeches and stockings, *"His legs were pointedly condemned by all the female connoisseurs of legs that I ever heard lecture on the topic."* But De Quincey calculated that those legs carried Wordsworth between 175,000 and 180,000 English miles much of which would have been across country in the Lake District where Wordsworth spent almost the whole of his life. And during many of those miles Wordsworth composed verse. His method of composition was to stride backwards and forwards, declaiming as he went: not for him the confines of a study or lamenting his lost love whilst reclining on a grassy knoll under the spreading branches of an ancient tree.

Shelley and Keats walked too and they will be met with again along the Trail.

Others reached Horsham. There was Arthur Beckett who looked forward to reaching it, *"for that is a place meet for high adventure"*.

Many today have cause, perhaps unknowingly, to be grateful to Arthur Beckett (1871-1943). Although born in Yorkshire he came to Sussex at an early age and developed a love for Sussex that was expressed in his writing and other ways. As first President of the South Downs Society (founded as the Society of Sussex Downsmen) he played a leading part in the struggle to protect and preserve the Downs. He was a journalist, founding Beckett Newspapers and also founding and editing the Sussex County Magazine. The Magazine survived until 1956; its back numbers are an invaluable source of reference. His books include *Spirit of the Downs* (1909), *The Wonderful Weald* (1911) and *Sussex at War and Poems of Peace* (1916).

The Wonderful Weald describes the quest of Beckett and Aminta, a portrayal of his wife Alice, through the Weald for the crock of gold at the end of the rainbow, the ends of which rested in the Weald. They were accompanied by the donkey that they hired to carry the baggage and christened Nick Bottom when they realised that they did not know his name. During the course of the journey they came to the *"honourable town of Horsham"* but they did not dwell overlong, their minds, perhaps, distracted by the tale of the Drewett brothers who had been hanged on Horsham Common in 1798 for robbery of His Majesty's Mail and that seems to be their sole memory of the town. There are happier stories elsewhere.

But William Cobbett preceded the Becketts to Horsham.

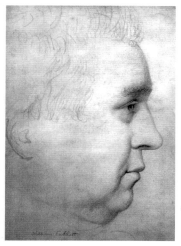

The name of William Cobbett (1762-1835) is hardly one with which to conjure today although the historian, the late A J P Taylor, considered him to be the runner up to Dr Samuel Johnson as the greatest Englishman. Although Cobbett's *Rural Rides* are a godsend to writers on the English countryside with many a trenchant comment, and trenchant they can be, he remains now little known in England. This applies equally to the United States where he first learned the art or craft of journalism and political pamphleteering during his stay in Philadelphia for some years from 1794. In the words of Richard Ingrams in his recent, aptly titled biography, *The Life and Adventures of William Cobbett* (2005), he developed into "*the most effective, most savage and most satirical political journalist of his or any other age.*"

The invective that modern politicians believe that they suffer pales into insignificance compared to that which Cobbett could, and did, heap upon an opponent. He also had a true sense of humour that probably made him even more unpopular with many a politician.

Born in Farnham in Surrey the third of four sons of a farmer who was also a one time innkeeper, Cobbett, not long turned twenty and dressed in his holiday clothes, was on his way to meet three girls to accompany them to Guildford Fair when the London stage coach came over the hill. On the spur of the moment Cobbett got on. Those adventures began in earnest.

Not more than half educated he furthered his education by voracious reading and intense private study, much during army service with the 54th Regiment of Foot. The regiment was posted to New Brunswick in Canada guarding the frontier with the United States in the years following the American War of Independence. He rose to the rank of sergeant major, being promoted over the heads of those more senior to him. His army career ended with his efforts to make public the corruption within the regiment. These backfired on him and led to the self imposed exile in Philadelphia. On his return to England in 1800, his name was already widely known from his writings whilst in America. His long career continued. Never dull, he was read even by those to whom he was opposed in the extreme.

A world-wide debt of gratitude is owed to him.

He furthered the freedom of the press. That included undergoing two years imprisonment for criminal libel. In those draconian and repressive days that charge, and the threat of it, was used by those in authority to gag adverse comment. The truth was no defence. And it was reaching a point when a trial would be an unnecessary luxury.

He promoted parliamentary reform when elections were mainly controlled by the few and rotten boroughs, where but a handful of electors, whose votes were controlled or could be bought, were a norm.

He was incorruptible with a horror of corruption neither seeking nor receiving favours in an age when corruption was rampant.

He was also an early proponent of what is now known as openness in government. He launched the reporting of proceedings in Parliament with *Cobbett's Parliamentary Debates*. He subsequently sold that business to the printer whose name was Hansard.

He was a man of indefatigable energy. In addition to his newspaper the *Political Register*, the collected edition of which is in eighty-eight volumes, his books cover a diverse range and include *A Grammar of the English Language* (1818), *Cottage Economy* (1821), *A French Grammar* (1824), *A History of the Protestant Reformation* (1824) and T*he English Gardener* (1828). He also farmed whenever he was able and never gave up his support for those who worked on the land.

He is best known for *Rural Rides* (1830). It was in the course of one of these that on 31st July 1823 he set off from Worth in Sussex at about 5 o'clock in the afternoon making for Horsham. He passed through Crawley, crossed the road to Brighton and came to "*six of the worst miles in England, which miles terminate but a few yards before you enter Horsham.*" He did, however, find Horsham to be "*... a very nice, solid, country town. Very clean, as all the towns in Sussex are. The people are very clean. The Sussex women are very nice in their dress and in their houses*".

Worth church

LEAVING HORSHAM

Our Trail begins from the 'Shelley Fountain' in the shopping precinct of Horsham. The fountain was designed by Angela Conner and its 'cosmic cycle' depicts how water influenced Shelley's life and untimely death. Each cycle involves the movement of an amazing six tons of water.

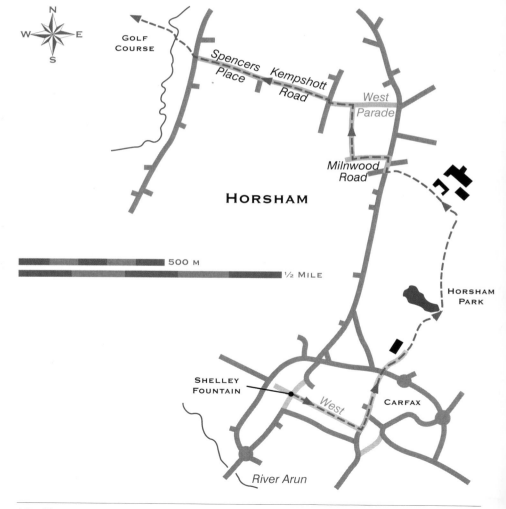

GOLF COURSE

Spencers Place

Kempshott Road

West Parade

Milnwood Road

HORSHAM

500 M

½ MILE

HORSHAM PARK

SHELLEY FOUNTAIN

West

CARFAX

River Arun

From the fountain head in an easterly direction along the pedestrianised West Street. At the top of the street, on meeting South Street & Middle Street and a wrought iron fingerpost, turn left following the sign towards the Post Office and walk into The Carfax.

Keep to the right of the Swan Walk shopping precinct and continue ahead along Medwin Walk. In a further 75m, take the subway under the main road. At the car park near the bowling alley, go straight ahead following the fingerpost towards 'Pavilions in the Park' onto a tarmac path across the park.

Pass the small lake to your left, and continue ahead following the sign to the 'Skate Board Park'. Stay on the tarmac path and in 300m, at a fork in the path by a metal barrier, (before the fire station) keep left to reach the northern corner of the park.

Exit through a gap in the high metal railings onto the public road and turn right. In 50m on reaching 'Parkfield' on the right cross the road carefully and take the first turning left down Milnwood Road. Just before reaching the end of this road turn right along Newlands Road and at the T-junction ahead turn left following the one-way sign.

At the next road cross straight over into Kempshott Road and walk ahead. This becomes Spencer's Place and crosses a rise to descend to another T-junction. Turn right and immediately left, before the telephone kiosk, following the public footpath and cycle track sign. Cross the stream ahead on a substantial wooden bridge and continue following footpath signs to right then left. Cross a larger brick bridge over the main stream from the millpond and walk ahead across the golf course. On reaching the next T-junction turn right following the sign to 'Warnham 1½ miles'.

Horsham to Barns Green

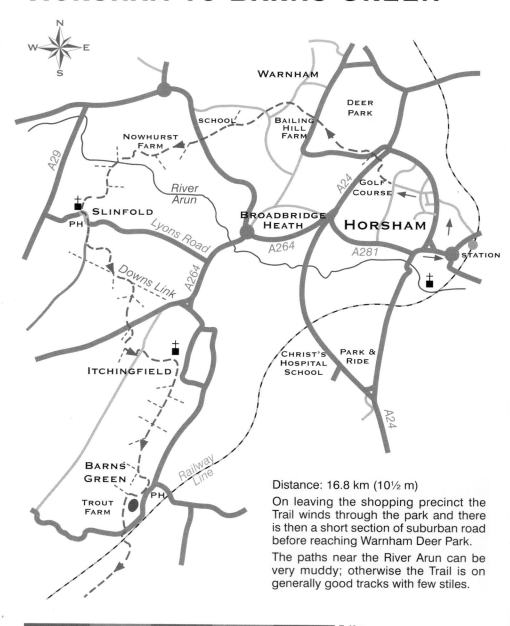

Distance: 16.8 km (10½ m)

On leaving the shopping precinct the Trail winds through the park and there is then a short section of suburban road before reaching Warnham Deer Park.

The paths near the River Arun can be very muddy; otherwise the Trail is on generally good tracks with few stiles.

5 KM

3 MILES

Old Gatehouse to Warnham Court

Pass under the A24 and follow the drive ahead to the public road. Continue ahead in the same direction, keeping to the right hand side of the road. Walk past 'Salmons' and in 500m turn right through a large metal kissing gate to enter Warnham Deer Park and follow the clearly defined path heading north westerly across the park.

As you pass the pond to your left the view to the right is of Warnham Court once the home of the Lucas Family who made their fortune in the early Victorian engineering industry building such landmarks as the Simplon Railway Tunnel, the original Aswan Dam and the Albert Hall. They extended the present house in the 1870s and lived here until 1947 when it was sold to the GLC and became a 'special needs' school. The school closed in March 1996 and the house has since been converted to luxury apartments. Warnham Park Estate continues to be owned by the Lucas family.

At the far side of the park pass through another kissing gate and cross the public road into Bailing Hill Farm. Walk through the farmyard with a timber framed house to your left.

This delightful building dates back to 1375. It was 'modernised' with the addition of a new frontage in the 18th century. You are now about to enter the

grazing paddocks for the 72-acre Bailing Hill Farm. This world-renowned stud deer farm supports a herd of 70 breeding hinds, 3 red deer sires and young stock. Valuable exports are made from here to Canada, New Zealand and many other parts of the world. It is vitally important that you disturb these beautiful creatures as little as possible and pass through quietly and gently.

Pass through the two large wire gates and begin walking slightly uphill. Pass through two more high kissing gates and follow the fencing on your right almost to the brow of the hill and then turn left, in front of the trees, to the higher corner of the field. There are views from here of Christ's Hospital, Horsham church spire and the South Downs. Pass through a very narrow kissing gate into a small wood and soon emerge through a wooden gate onto a public road. Turn right and then immediately left over a stile following the footpath sign down a pleasant broad track between two hedges.

At the next road cross straight over through a gateway and walk across the field ahead. Turn half right at the corner of the tennis court following the fingerpost with a large open field to the left. At the far corner of the wood look carefully for a fingerpost directing you to the right, heading towards farm buildings, and in just 20m on reaching a T-junction with a bridleway, turn left.

At the bottom of the dip pass a large lake to your left and turn left over a stile. On reaching the brow of a small rise turn half right into an enclosed path with an open field to the left.

The building you see to your right is Farlington School – a day and boarding school for 500 girls aged from 4 to 18. The official foundation of Farlington School was in 1896. The school moved to its present site in 1955, where it occupies 33 acres of beautiful parkland. There are two lakes, sports and recreational facilities and a small farm within the grounds.

Walk past the school on your right to the busy main road. Cross into Nowhurst Lane following the bridleway sign. At the next bridleway junction keep right following the tarmac drive past Old Strood Coach House.

Note the Horsham stone roofing on Smithawe Farm. This attractive but extremely heavy slate probably came from nearby Slinfold where it was extensively quarried. The sheer weight of the roof requires a substantial frame to support it and Horsham stone is always a good indication that the building is probably timber-framed, as this one clearly is.

In a further 700m at Nowhurst Farm keep initially right, as the tarmac drive becomes gravel, and then in 15m swing left to pass through a metal gate onto a broad enclosed track between two paddocks. At the end of the paddocks reach an open field and turn left downhill, then swing right to follow the path around the bottom of the field. On reaching a three-fingered post, with a line of tall trees to the right, turn left across a concrete bridge over the river.

This is the fledgling River Arun, the second fastest flowing river in England (it speeds up a bit further on!). One of only four major rivers in West Sussex, it rises in St Leonard's Forest and flows out to sea at Littlehampton just south of the old port of Arundel. Our Trail crosses it again as it cuts through the Downs at Houghton Bridge.

Turn right to follow the river for 200m and reach a fingerpost indicating a footpath heading uphill to the left. Turn left and walk over the hill to join the tarmac drive leading downhill away from Rowfold Farmhouse.

The farm covers 170 acres, most of which are cultivated. The present owners have introduced some wonderful conservation measures. These include ten metre strips of land beside the river banks being left uncultivated to provide premium wildlife habitat and a low lying meadow besides the river being maintained as a wilderness refuge for wildlife. Crops recommended by the RSPB are grown in selected areas of the farm, adjacent to hedges, to provide optimum habitat for bird life and an otter holt has been built in a discrete river bank location. Not surprisingly, there have been recent sightings of otters on the farm.

At the bottom of the hill, just before the buildings, turn right following the footpath towards the church. 50m into the graveyard fork left to reach the entrance to St Peter's Church, Slinfold.

The church is normally open and is well worth a visit. Despite being relatively modern (the present church dates from 1861 and the tower from 1970)

it houses some wonderful treasures and information about them is well displayed inside. Nairn and Pevsner, described the church as 'proud and uncompromising but not unsympathetic'.

Bear left before reaching the porch to go through a gate by the village hall onto the main road and turn left past the war memorial towards the Red Lyon public house.

The earliest reference to this building is in 1513 when it was known as Nibletts. The first mention of it being an inn or alehouse comes in 1687 when it was called The Red Lyon although court records dating back to the 1630s show a John Penfold of Slinfold being fined for selling illegal measures! Sometime between then and the mid 1800s its name was changed to the 'Kings Head'. Thankfully the original name has now been restored.

Slinfold is a very pretty village with some fine Georgian houses. One of Slinfold's most important local industries was the quarrying of Horsham stone. It was once carried by river barge from around Slinfold to the sea, and then on to its many final destinations. The quarries are now exhausted and replacing broken stones is a major problem.

Where the main road swings left, turn right down Hayes Lane and in 300m, immediately after passing the mini roundabout at 'Six Acres', look for a fingerpost on the left indicating a footpath besides a wooden fence. Turn left down the gravel path and walk through the housing estate for 250m to reach a small pond. Swing right with the path and at the end of the panelled fencing, where there is an open space, meet a crossing path and turn left following the fingerpost over a plank bridge and stile. Turn half right, with the fence line now on your left, to reach a stile and the 'Downs Link'.

The 'Downs Link' is a 37-mile bridleway linking the North Downs Way at Guildford with the South Downs Way at Bramber. For most of its route it follows two disused railway lines and is, as you would therefore expect, fairly straight and level and perhaps better suited to cycling rather than walking. It has been described as a 'green corridor' passing almost unnoticed through many villages.

Turn left along the 'Link' and in 500 m, at the first crossing path, turn right over a stile and walk up the right hand side of the field, keeping strictly to the field edge, to the far right corner. Pass through a metal gate and continue ahead uphill into woodland. Cross a stile besides a metal gate on your left into an open field and climb ahead through two more farm gates, keeping clear of the trees to your right. At the top of the rise cross a stile besides another gate and reach a gravel drive; cross diagonally over the drive into a path between the trees with dense rhododendron bushes to the right and emerge onto the busy Toat Hill Road.

Ignoring the bridleway directly opposite, turn half left for 10m and look for a public footpath sign crossing a stile onto a narrow, enclosed path heading southeast. On reaching a tarmac drive besides Toat Copse turn right and in 175m pass through a metal gate and immediately turn left, before reaching Lower Toat Farm, along a broad drive heading slightly uphill.

At the public road ahead turn left and in 50m turn right at the entrance to 'The Warren'. Almost immediately bear left off the drive to follow the narrow footpath through a small gate. At the end of this path cross a stile and walk downhill across the centre of a large open field with fine views of Horsham in the distance. At the bottom of the field cross a stile and a substantial wooden footbridge to enter a small copse.

Ignoring a fingerpost left, continue ahead and on leaving the copse cross a plank bridge and stile and climb the steep bank uphill towards the church. Turn right over the stile into the churchyard.

Itchingfield church dates back to 1125; it has a fine early Norman window still surviving and a particular feature of the church is its Medieval Bell Tower. The unique 'Priest's House' in the grounds of the church dates from the15th century and was used as an almshouse in the 19th century.

Pass between the porch and the Priest's House to the wide entrance drive; walk up to the main road and turn right. Where the road swings left, in front of the primary school, keep straight ahead ignoring the 'private' sign and follow this public right of way. In 600m pass through the wooden gate besides Muntham Lodge.

In a further 500m reach a wooden gate to Muntham House School where there is a 3-armed fingerpost. Take the path half left through a gap in the railing and follow a feint track through the woods just to the left side of the playing fields.

In the 1800s Percy Godman bought The Muntham Estate and rebuilt the house you see. He lived the life of a Victorian country gentleman with many servants and employees, who all needed somewhere to live. This and the coming of the railway brought about the expansion of Barns Green. The house is now occupied by Muntham House School which was established in 1953 as an educational trust, set up to offer educational support for boys and young men who were unable to learn in mainstream education.

The path will eventually emerge onto the edge of the playing fields and in another 100m as you near the main house of the school will re-enter the woods and lead down to a stile onto a tarmac road. Turn left heading downhill to pass the village hall of Barns Green and at the main road cross carefully and turn right to the Queens Head.

This was originally the Bricklayer's Arms but had become the Queen's Head by 1852. When innkeepers moved on they often took the name of their previous establishment with them, which accounts for some of these name changes throughout history. It is a timber-framed building of the 1600s, which

was cased in the more fashionable brick in the 19th. century. A favourite pastime in these parts was that of 'Skug Hunting' – the pursuit of squirrels, which was traditionally practised in the woods of the parish on Boxing Day. These days they settle for more traditional celebrations.

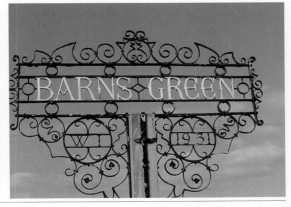

ON THE WAY

It is a truth universally acknowledged that an author in possession of a manuscript, must be in want of a publisher. But like marriage, the relationship was, and is, not always easy. Money is often the obstacle in either relationship. John Murray, Byron's publisher, sent Byron a luxurious edition of a bible in return for a favour, perhaps not entirely an appropriate gift for Byron. It was returned with *"Now Barabbas was a robber"* altered to *"Now Barabbas was a publisher."*

Alexander Pope (1699-1744), the great 18th century poet, also had complaints about his publisher, Bernard Lintot, who makes some fleeting appearances in Pope's works and who on one occasion Pope described as a 'scoundrel' resolving never to employ him again, although they appear to be in contact at the time of Lintot's death in 1736.

Bernard Barnaby Lintot was born on 1st December 1675 in the village of Southwater close to Horsham. He became a bookseller in London where he developed into the foremost bookseller of the first third of the 18th century. Like other booksellers of his age he progressed into publishing where he played a significant part in the development of English literature. In addition to Pope, his authors included Dryden, Congreve and Gay. Also very significant was his publication of Pope's translation into English of Homer's *Iliad*. For the first time illustrations were used that related to the text rather than being just decorations on the page.

Alexander Pope had other connections with the Horsham area. The house is no longer there but his great friend, John Caryll, lived at West Grinstead Park where the young Hornungs were later to live across the road from Mrs Conan Doyle. There it is said Pope sat beneath an oak tree and wrote *The Rape of the Lock* (1714) in 1712. This is remembered at Pope's Oak Farm, the sign for which stands beside the A272 at West Grinstead.

Pope was not averse to patronising the second biggest industry in 18th century Sussex after agriculture: smuggling. In an episode reminiscent of the modern *"something falling off the back of a lorry"* he wrote to John Caryll in August 1717. He reported having completed a errand for his friend and continued,

"As I have discharged this small office for you, I beg you to do me a familiar or rather domestic piece of service. It is, when a hogshead of good French wine falls into your hands – whether out of the skies, or whatever element that pays no customs – that you would favour me with about twelve dozen of it at the price you give."

Lintot left Horsham but John Baker (1712-79) came to the town. A barrister by profession and a wealthy man through marriage, he retired to Horsham in 1771 and joined the ranks of the Horsham diarists. In his diary he was much concerned with his health, the weather, attending trials in court at the Guildhall in London and, above all, cricket. His diary is a major source for the contemporary cricket scene and, in some ways, there has been little change since. There were the equivalent of hospitality boxes where the hospitality enjoyed overtook interest in the game: spectators rioted, there were heroic performances (and the reverse), substantial wagers were placed. But change was also then taking place. The middle stump was added to the wicket following a match from which John Baker was driven by riot. After he left, the bowling of 'Lumpy' Stevens beat an outstanding batsman three times, only to pass without effect through the centre of the open wicket. It was also a time when the width of the bat was regulated following another occasion when a batsman came to the crease with a bat wider than the wicket.

On 4th August 1792 Percy Bysshe Shelley was born close to Horsham at Field Place, Warnham, the first child of Timothy and Elizabeth Shelley.

Shelley is an old name in the Sussex aristocracy but the Shelleys at Field Place were somewhat distant cousins and had arrived at titles and land via America. The newly born Shelley's great-grandfather, another Timothy, a younger son who would not inherit, had been forced to emigrate to America to try to make a living. It seems that he failed as a merchant and became a quack doctor instead. His son, Bysshe, the poet's grandfather, was born in Newark, New Jersey in 1731. A fortunate family inheritance later enabled the family to return to England. Shelley's grandfather seems to have acquired the American drive that led to the family fortunes. He founded a family tradition that the poet was to follow by eloping with and marrying young women, who would now be called teenagers. In his case it was heiresses, both of whom died before him leaving him with their estates including Field Place. The young poet was to follow the tradition save that neither of his brides, one of whom was to outlive him, were propertied. Bysshe, the grandfather became a baronet in 1806. He died in 1815 when the title passed to Sir Timothy, the poet's father, who, by then, was estranged from his eldest son.

Shelley was born into a world of turmoil, revolution, war, social unrest: the old order under attack and resisting. His childhood, however, can be described as idyllic. There were fields to roam and woods to explore. There was Warnham Pond to learn to sail. There was a growing band of sisters to lead on walks, one of their destinations being Strood House a mile or so away from Field Place. Strood House is now Farlington School and the Trail passes close by, literally cutting across where Shelley and his sisters must have walked.

There were also tales fantastical to be told to his sisters of his adventures and of horror, magic and monsters, including the Great Tortoise that lived in Warnham Pond and of the Alchemist, old and grey. There was a taste for experimentation and for raising fire. There were the signs of the imagination that would serve the poet

Strood House – compare with how it looks today as Farlington School on page 14.

but not of the genius that was to flourish nor of the extreme political radical that he was to become.

The rural idyll largely ended when he was sent away to school. First Syon House Academy at Isleworth and then on to Eton. He was no longer the leader of a compliant band but an individual who stood apart from his peers: the object of intense bullying that he met with a violent temper often deliberately provoked by his tormentors for their amusement. A temper that he was to carry into later life. His overwhelming hatred of injustice must have been brought out by his schooldays.

During the holidays there were still the stories to be told and experiments to be carried out that widened in range and depth as his physical and mental horizons expanded: ghost raising, chemistry, electricity, explosions, alchemy, and psychical investigations.

From Eton, where finally he appears to have created an eccentric niche for himself, he went on to Oxford in 1810. He went with the advice from his father that his father would provide for as many natural children as he (young Shelley) chose to have but that he would never be forgiven for making a mésalliance. Advice that Shelley was to disregard not once but twice, which undoubtedly contributed to the estrangement from his family and the opprobrium in which he was held by his contemporaries.

At Oxford the experiments continued. In his rooms there was a welter of scientific and electrical equipment, books, clothing, pistols and broken crockery over a carpet stained by chemicals and apparently singed by fire. More seriously, in an age and at an institution of staunch Christianity, he and his friend, Thomas Jefferson Hogg, published a pamphlet, *The Necessity of Atheism* (1811) printed in Worthing. It may have been the first printed open avowal of atheism in England. It led to their expulsion from the university.

For a while Shelley returned to Field Place but ultimately the terms under which his father would allow him to remain, were unacceptable to Shelley and his terms were unacceptable to his father. His wanderings were beginning and his direct contact with Sussex was coming to an end. His radical (extreme left as we would now say) and egalitarian views and political pamphleteering were coming to the fore. The Home Office opened a file on his subversive activities.

In 1811, not yet twenty, Shelley eloped to Edinburgh and married Harriet Westbrook with whom his sisters had been at school. She was 16 years old when earlier in the year Shelley, in his loneliness, began to rely on the company of her and her sisters. As the daughter of a retired merchant and coffee-house proprietor, albeit an affluent one, she did not match Timothy Shelley's standards. Three years later in 1814 Shelley met the 16 year old Mary Godwin and eloped with her to Switzerland; her half-sister went with them. Shelley did write to Harriet urging her to come to Switzerland and become a member of the community that he hoped to establish although he did not remain long enough to do so. Shelley married Mary two years later in 1816 when he became free to do so following Harriet's suicide by drowning in the Serpentine in London earlier that year. Shelley's application to the Court for custody of his children with Harriet failed. He was awarded strictly limited visiting rights but there is no evidence that he ever exercised these.

It was on a trip to Switzerland in 1816 during a spell of bad weather when Shelley and Lord Byron were unable to sail that it was proposed that some among the party should each tell a ghost story. From this, and inspired by a nightmare, Mary Shelley created Frankenstein and wrote the novel. There are misconceptions about Frankenstein. Frankenstein is the creator, not the monster. It was he who made a creature that is far removed from the Hollywood monster with its visible stitching

"When I placed my head upon my pillow, I did not sleep, nor could I be said to think...I saw – with shut eyes, but acute mental vision – I saw the pale student of unhallowed arts kneeling beside the thing he had put together." Mary Shelley.

and a bolt though its neck. The creature is described as having limbs in proportion and with beautiful features.

Shelley's biographer, Richard Holmes, draws attention to the parallels between the educations of Shelley and Frankenstein, places visited by and known to Shelley and Frankenstein and common incidents and experiences. He also writes, *"Implicitly, Shelley accepted his own identification as Frankenstein's monster."* It seems, therefore, that Frankenstein and his monster both walked the fields of Sussex and that their paths crossed our Trail.

Shelley was to die in a sailing accident off the coast of Italy in 1822 a few weeks short of his thirtieth birthday. Again in the words of his biographer, Richard Holmes, *"At the time of his death his reputation was almost literally unspeakable in England, an object to be torn apart between the conservative and radical* reviews, but not on the whole to be mentioned in polite London society." This was an attitude to linger in the long local memories in and about Horsham even after the more widespread sanitization of Shelley by his widow and her daughter-in-law so that he became a poet of romance rather than the rebel and rampant political force that he was.

Unlike Lord Byron, Shelley enjoyed little financial reward from his poetry. Perhaps it was because of this and the life of his elder son that Sir Timothy Shelley offered two pieces of advice. To his younger son, *"Never read a book, Johnnie, and you will be a rich man"* and, perhaps to the world at large, *"My son writes books, and no gentleman does that."*

But Shelley had also been a walker when no gentleman did that either. Shelley's friend, Thomas Hogg, described Shelley as being well-suited *"to perform, as it were, a pedestrian steeplechase"*.

Walking was partly for pleasure and partly from necessity when he had no funds to pay for transport. It included walking south from Paris for five days on that elopement in 1814 with the 16 year old Mary Godwin and Mary's sister. They covered some thirty miles a day although a mule did carry their luggage.

From about 1930 Georgette Heyer (1902-1974) and her husband ran a sports shop at Horsham. She was a prolific writer who published more than 50 books over a working life of more than 50 years: some had Sussex settings or contained Sussex scenes. There were 40 historical novels, 12 crime novels and 4 contemporary novels. For a while they lived at Colgate just outside Horsham but, in 1932, the family moved to a house near Slinfold, a village through which the Trail passes. It was at Slinfold that Georgette Heyer wrote her first crime novel and her best known historical novel, *Regency Buck* (1935), set in the period with which she is most associated. She wrote to support her husband and family whilst he studied to become a barrister: willingly in her case unlike other women writers who had the need to support a family thrust upon them. The family moved from the area in 1939 when her husband qualified, at first to Brighton to ease commuting to London and later to London itself.

Following the Trail southwards there are glimpses over to the left of the water tower of Christ's Hospital, the Bluecoat School. The school was founded in 1552 by King Edward VI, the short lived son of Henry VIII, as a charity to educate the poor children of London. It still retains its original ethos although it now spreads its net wider than London. About 25-30% of the students come from London, about 30% from Sussex with

the remainder from all over Britain and the world. Out of some 800 students only 3% pay full fees: 40% pay none at all.

The school removed to Horsham from the City of London in 1902. There is a history of the progression of its removal in the works of E V Lucas (1868-1939) who we will meet again along the Trail. In a note to the 1902 edition of the *Essays*

of Elia that he edited, Lucas wrote that "*the school is about to be removed from London.*" In the 1904 first edition of his *Highways & Byways of Sussex* Lucas referred to the "*new Christ's Hospital*" that had "*been built in the midst of green fields; an arrogant red-brick town which the fastidiously urban ghost of Charles Lamb can never visit.*" In the 1923 pocket edition of *Highways & Byways in Sussex* Lucas added the words, "*'Lamb's House' however, is the name of one of the buildings; and Time the Healer,*

who can do all things, may mellow the new school into Elian congeniality." The school celebrated its centenary at Horsham in 2002 and may, perhaps, be described as having mellowed.

Christ's Hospital has a long literary tradition. The "*fastidiously urban*" Charles Lamb was at the school in the late 18th century. His contemporary was Samuel Taylor Coleridge and they remained friends afterwards. But that was before the school came to Horsham and their work is outside even the elastic boundaries of the Trail. The literary tradition, however, has continued at Horsham particularly with two war poets, one from each of the two World Wars.

Edmund Blunden (1896-1974), poet, biographer, literary critic, soldier and scholar, was educated at Christ's Hospital which he was attending in 1914 when the First World War broke out. He enlisted and by 1915 had been commissioned as a second lieutenant in the 11th battalion of the Royal Sussex Regiment known as the 1st South Downs Battalion. He fought at Ypres and the Somme, where he was awarded the Military Cross. Almost miraculously he survived until the end of the war but, like all soldiers who serve in such 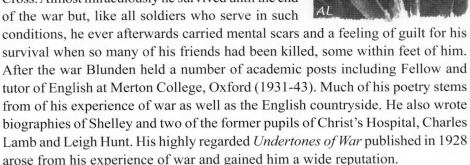 conditions, he ever afterwards carried mental scars and a feeling of guilt for his survival when so many of his friends had been killed, some within feet of him. After the war Blunden held a number of academic posts including Fellow and tutor of English at Merton College, Oxford (1931-43). Much of his poetry stems from of his experience of war as well as the English countryside. He also wrote biographies of Shelley and two of the former pupils of Christ's Hospital, Charles Lamb and Leigh Hunt. His highly regarded *Undertones of War* published in 1928 arose from his experience of war and gained him a wide reputation.

Keith Douglas (1920-1944) was a poet and painter whose painting might have predominated if he had lived. He was able to attend Christ's Hospital through the charitable nature of the school where he was difficult, but flourished: the first poem in a later published collection was written when he was fourteen. In 1938 he entered Merton College, Oxford, where Blunden was tutor, to read English: Blunden immediately recognised his promise. Douglas enlisted on the outbreak of the second World War in 1939 but was deferred until 1940. He was commissioned in 1941 and served in tanks: first in North Africa where he was wounded, and later as part of the main assault in the Normandy D Day landings on 6th June 1944. He was killed three days later. He died a recognised and published poet who was prevented from reaching the fullness of his promise. His work was almost lost to notice but for inclusion in anthologies; several collected and selected editions have now been published.

It is not that the deaths of war poets are more tragic than the loss of life around them but that they, and those who survive, are better able to articulate the effects and waste of war.

BARNS GREEN TO NUTBOURNE

Walk down Chapel Road to pass the Queens Head and post office on your left and in a further 200m, at the entrance to Slaughterford Farm, turn right onto a broad open track with a barn on the left. At the first finger post turn left through a metal farm gate into an open field,

and follow the path to the right of a small lake. Reach a gate into the woods and follow the woodland path to a tarmac drive. Turn left and follow the drive to the main road.

Cross the road with care and turn right. In just 25m turn left following the bridleway sign through a metal gate and over a stile, to carefully cross the railway line. Follow the path ahead as it swings right and in about 250m reach Ballbrook House Farm. Keep to the right of the large house following the gravel drive between two hedges and upon reaching the metal gates of the house, besides a pillar box, keep right again to pass through a gate. Continue ahead, with the timber-framed house on your left, and pass through two more gates to reach a concrete drive with an open field to the right and Lower Pratts Farm ahead. Ignoring the footpath on the left, bear right at the house to pass through another gate and reach a driveway.

This area has a pleasant wet, woody character and the settlements tend to be small and scattered, sometimes just a line of houses along an old transport corridor through the Weald. The majority of the buildings are traditional in character with orange-red brick and clay hung tiles reflecting the use of local Weald clays and providing attractive contrast with the vivid green vegetation. Many of the older buildings are half-timbered with greeny-grey Horsham Stone roofs.

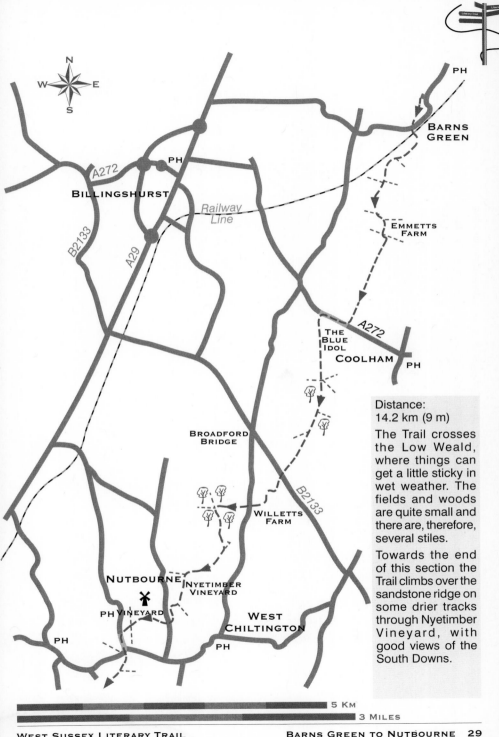

Distance:
14.2 km (9 m)

The Trail crosses the Low Weald, where things can get a little sticky in wet weather. The fields and woods are quite small and there are, therefore, several stiles.

Towards the end of this section the Trail climbs over the sandstone ridge on some drier tracks through Nyetimber Vineyard, with good views of the South Downs.

5 KM

3 MILES

Continue along the driveway and after about 250m, as the driveway swings right, continue straight ahead into light woodland. Emerge from these woods through a gate into an open field. Part way along this field look for a bridleway fingerpost to the right. Turn right and then immediately left so that the open field is now to your right. Pass through gateways and descend to the bottom of the dip. Passing beneath the power lines turn half left to climb the rise ahead diagonally across the field. At the top of the field pass through a gateway to a 4-fingered post and a rough drive.

Turn left, following the bridleway sign along the drive, and in 200m when this drive begins to swing left towards farm buildings, continue straight ahead following the bridleway fingerpost with the tree line on your left. This reaches a T-junction with a bridleway to the left and a footpath to the right. Turn left keeping to the bridleway and, before reaching the gardens of the farmhouse, turn right again on the bridleway route. After about 150m pass through a gateway with an open field now to the right and the hedgeline to your left. In the far corner of this field turn right and in just 20m turn left into woodland. Cross over a small stream and emerge into an open field with a tree line to your left.

You are now in the heart of the 'Low Weald' of West Sussex, a low lying, gently undulating area of ponds and small streams, often with wet woodlands of alder and willow. The name derives from the Anglo-Saxon word 'wald' meaning forest and in the Domesday Book of 1086 it is recorded that two-thirds of this land was densely forested. The hedgerows tend to be tall with many mature trees running between small copses – once used to provide charcoal for local iron and glass production.

There is abundant wildlife here and woodland birds such as nuthatch and tree creeper are particularly common, as are deer and badgers. In late April many of the woods are covered with carpets of wild hyacinth – better known as the English Bluebell. They flower with up to 12 heads on a juicy stem. The six separate petals curl outwards at the tip and the prolific carpet they produce is one of the most beautiful seasonal sights in England. For this reason they are never picked.

At the far corner of this field go ahead across a concrete bridge through a gateway. Bear right following a track onto a much broader grassy ride. At the end of the ride go through a narrow gateway and continue uphill following a hedgeline on your right. At the top of this rise pass through a gateway and continue ahead to the main road.

On reaching the main road, opposite Haymans Ghyll, cross carefully to the pavement opposite and turn right to walk past Snow Hill Farm and Hayler's. After about 500m, as the road swings right, turn left into Old House Lane. In a further 400m reach the entrance to the Blue Idol on your left.

The oldest parts of this delightful timber framed farmhouse date from around 1580. In 1691 a galleried room was created by the removal of two bays of the first floor in the south wing. This was the Quaker Meeting House, which

William Penn attended regularly. He lived for over 30 years at Warminghurst, just 4 miles away, and would often ride here on horseback, whilst his wife and children came by coach. It was at Warminghurst that Penn, with the help of Algernon Sidney, drafted the Constitution of Pennsylvania. The unusual name does not appear until the late 19th century. The house had been colour-washed in blue and was

QUAKER
AND FOUNDER
OF PENNSYLVANIA
WILLIAM PENN
1644 – 1718
WITH OTHER FRIENDS
HE ESTABLISHED THIS
MEETING HOUSE
WEST SUSSEX COUNTY COUNCIL

closed for 76 years. It may therefore simply have been a 'blue, idle house' – the word idle was often used at that time for any unoccupied building. The Blue Idol is now an active Quaker Meeting House and welcomes visitors of any faith.

After leaving the Blue Idol continue ahead southwards on the driveway for 500m to pass Old House Farm and a barn conversion. Keep straight ahead as the bridleway narrows into the woods and walk through a short section which can be rather waterlogged at times. Go through a metal gate and in 200m ignore a bridleway left and walk ahead for a further 500m to reach two derelict barns on the right. Ignore the footpath to the right and continue ahead on the narrow bridleway through the trees. In a further 900m reach a main road and cross carefully to a grassy area opposite. Turn half left to an old wooden gate and a finger post. Pass through the gate and follow the track beneath the power lines. At the T-junction turn right and follow a rough and sometimes muddy track through light woodland to emerge at Willetts Farm and a public road.

Many of the houses here are timber-framed and we find two distinctive styles in West Sussex. The first is known most appropriately as a 'Wealden'. These mainly 15th century buildings had an open hall for the full height of the house. The smoke from the fire on the floor of the family room would find its way out through small gables at the top of the roof. At both ends was a two-storey section for sleeping. They had a distinctive elevation, with great curved

braces in the central recessed section partly supporting the roof and at each end of these braces was a jetty or projecting first floor. A little later the jetty became a full feature along the front elevation, which provided more accommodation on the first floor and omitted the full height hall. This second style of house was known as 'Continuous Jetty'.

The great iron industry of the Weald demanded vast quantities of wood and diminishing timber resources brought about a further gradual change of style. The ground floor timbers of many of the old framed houses were suffering from rising damp and benefited from being infilled with fashionable brickwork from the new 'brick & tile' industries of Sussex.

Cross directly over the road to enter the driveway opposite. Pass Gables Farm and Blount's Cottage on the right and reach a gateway by the horse stables. Continue ahead into the wood. Ignore a prominent but unmarked crossing path and continue to the next one where there is a 4-armed fingerpost. Turn left following the bridleway sign through the woods. Emerge from the woods to the left hand side of a large open field and continue straight ahead following the left hand field boundary. 15m before the far left hand corner of this field turn left through a metal gate into the woods, following the public bridleway sign, and in just 15m turn half right following the footpath fingerpost going uphill into the trees through a wooden barrier.

You are now walking through a grove of Sweet or Spanish Chestnut trees. They are grown more extensively on the continent for their delicious nutty fruit, which can be cooked, preserved or ground into flour. The timber itself is little used now except, with a combination of willow, in the making of those wonderful, traditional 'Sussex Trug' baskets.

The Horse Chestnut is from a quite different family. It is not a native tree but was imported from Greece and Bulgaria to grace our parks and avenues. In late April the white, yellow and deep pink flowers blossom to give a beautiful 'lighted Christmas tree' effect. Its fruit, of course, is the inedible 'conker'.

The footpath passes through another wooden barrier to reach a sunken bridleway and here turn half right to continue uphill. Continue following the bridleway through two metal gates to reach the top of the rise. Just before the bridleway bears sharp left look for a finger post on the right. Take this footpath across a stile into an open field. Follow the finger post diagonally across this large level field towards a mid point half way along the tree line on the far side. On reaching the tree line turn right and follow the line of trees to an unusual stile besides a gate. Continue ahead with the vines of Nyetimber Vineyard to your left.

Nestling quietly in its own Sussex valley, Nyetimber is a magnificent half-timbered manor house dating back to Saxon times. Mentioned in the Domesday Book, it was once the home of Anne of Cleves, who acquired the house as part of her divorce settlement with Henry VIII. There is a minstrel's gallery in the double-height drawing room and a snug, panelled dining room. The estate has its own spring-fed lake.

The vines were first planted back in 1988 entirely with Chardonnay and a sparkling wine produced four years later. The 35 acres of gentle, south-facing slopes of greensand soil are now planted with Chardonnay, Pinot Noir and Pinot Meunier, the classic varieties of the Champagne region, and produce exceptional and highly praised sparkling wines. They have been served at many high profile events including the 2005 International Olympic Committee dinner at Buckingham Palace. Oz Clarke, in typical fashion, claims "Nyetimber 1996 Blanc de Blancs will blast most champagnes out of the water!"

The path emerges into the main vineyard buildings where there is a crossing bridleway. Here turn left following the bridleway sign with the delightful Manor House to your right. After about 450m, on reaching a group of houses, bear right following the sweep of the drive. About 50m before reaching the lane ahead, turn left into the entrance to Nyetimber Farm and then immediately right up a bank. Follow the enclosed path around the perimeter of the bungalow to turn left at the corner and then follow the right hand field boundary gently downhill with fine views across the golf course to the South Downs. In about 250m. reach a fingerpost T-junction and turn right down steps into the lane. Cross straight over with care and enter the driveway to Stile Farm Cottage. Walk up the gravel drive between the house and open garage and follow

the narrow footpath to the left of the yew hedge. This leads to a metal gate into an open field. Follow the right hand hedge line passing through several gates along the side of the field to reach Stuart's Wood.

'Stuarts Wood' is named after Stuart Brown, an author who loved this land and grew good asparagus here for nearly 20 years. His family planted these trees here in 2003 with the aid of a grant from the Forestry Commission. The plantation is 'natural' in that it comprises broad leaf trees similar to those found locally: Oak, Ash. Hornbeam, Field Maple, Lime etc.

There is free, open access to the whole wood. With only a small fraction of the woodland we had in southern Britain 200 years ago, even small sites such as this are vital to reducing carbon dioxide in the atmosphere; lessening the risk of flooding and absorbing chemicals from agricultural land before they get into the water system. It all helps.

The derelict mill to the right is the visitor centre for Nutbourne Vineyards, open to the public from May to October. This independent vineyard has 18 acres planted with five different grape varieties giving distinctive and award-winning dry white wines. If the centre is open do drop in and try a glass of their splendid 'Sussex Oak'.

The walk continues ahead between the vines to reach the attractive stone mill house. Now look carefully to the right of the house for a narrow path on your left. Follow this across the millstream and around the rear of the

house. At the end of the first lake turn right up the bank to cross a stile into an open field. Follow the hedge line on the right and, at the far side of the field, cross a stile and turn right then left to emerge onto The Street in Nutbourne. Turn left to continue following the Trail southwards out of the village – or turn briefly right to reach the Rising Sun.

Southwards Towards the Downs

From Horsham, William Cobbett, and a century later the Becketts, went on to Billingshurst, a village two miles away north west along the A272 from where the Trail crosses it; and that road should not be overlooked on a literary Trail. It has an ode addressed to it: *A272: An Ode to a Road* by Pieter Boogarts first published in 2000.

At Billingshurst Cobbett found "*A very pretty village, and a very nice breakfast, in a very neat little parlour of a very decent public-house*" and the landlady's young son in his blue smock reminded Cobbett of himself at that age. The Becketts were not quite so fortunate. "*Now when we had passed Horsham it so happened that a certain evil spirit led us in the direction of Billingshurst; and in this you are to note that I say no evil of Billingshurst itself.*" Dallying on the way, they were short of Billingshurst without lodging for the night and were directed "*to a certain roadside hostelry.*" "*But of the quality of that shelter and food I will say nothing, only praying that the self-same evil spirit that directed us to this inn, will direct thereto my worst enemy when he comes upon that road.*"

E V (Edward Verrall) Lucas (1868-1938) has already made an appearance on the Trail and will make others along the way. Although he was born in Kent, he was brought to Sussex so soon afterwards that he counted himself as a "*loyal South Saxon.*" He left school when he was sixteen to become apprenticed to a Brighton bookseller but he deeply regretted not having a wider, classical education due to the unpredictability of his father's finances. At twenty one he joined the *Sussex Daily News* as a reporter and published his first volume of poetry, *Sparks from a Flint*, in the following year. A gift of £200 from an uncle who was impressed by his literary skill and who wished him to advance his career, enabled him to go to London to attend lectures at University College where he also read widely. In 1893 when funds were on the point of running out he was recruited to The Globe, a leading evening newspaper, continuing his voracious reading at the British Museum Reading Room Library that he was later to describe as his *"real Alma Mater."* Soon afterwards he received his first commission for a book from the Society of Friends (the Quakers) for a memoir of Bernard Barton, a Quaker poet, who had been a friend of Charles Lamb for whom, with *"his supreme sense and nonsense"*, Lucas already had a profound admiration. This led to a commission from the publisher, Methuen, for a new edition of Lamb that ran to seven volumes and a biography. Lucas's reputation was established.

According to one source, he had some 180 books to his credit: travel, romances, humour, biographies, essays, poetry, children's books and anthologies. He had expertise in cricket, Pekinese dogs, Japanese scrolls and Chinese rice-paper books. In 1903 he was invited to join Punch, the great comic magazine that had been founded in 1841. He stayed for thirty years. At the same time he was not only being published, he was also publishing, rising to become the Chairman of Methuen in 1924.

In Sussex he is best known for the volume *Sussex* in the Highways & Byways series first published in the early 1900s. His first exercise in, to use his own words, *"anecdotal topography"*, *Highways & Byways in Sussex* was first published in 1904. There was a second edition in 1935 that was reprinted in 1950. As already seen at Christ's Hospital the book records passing changes. In 1904 Lucas referred to a visitor suddenly alighting in Sussex from a balloon. In 1935 that had become an aeroplane. With more relevance to the walker, he recalled in the preface to the 1935 edition that the most noticeable change was that in 1904 when motoring was in its infancy the roads were still their centuries old yellow and much dusty in dry weather: not the slate colour that they had become and are today.

In *Reading, Writing and Remembering* (1932), he explored the highways and byways of the literary scene for much of his life giving glimpses of books and authors some of whose titles and names remain familiar and others, who although well received in their day, have passed into obscurity.

During his life he paid for the upkeep of Charles Lamb's grave and on his death left money so that might continue in perpetuity.

The South Downs become clearer as the Trail continues southwards with sights of Chanctonbury Ring, still many years from full recovery from the devastating hurricane in 1987: here the Reverend Francis Kilvert (1840-79), away from his parish to attend a wedding at Worthing, fell in love with Kathleen Mavourneen. *"Chanctonbury, sweet Chanctonbury, thou wilt always be a green and beautiful spot in my memory."* (Kilvert's Diary 11th August 1874). But, in spite of his hopes at the time, he was to marry another.

Another churchman who came under the spell of the South Downs and Chanctonbury Ring in particular was Mervyn Stockwood (1913-95), sometime Bishop of Southwark. He was no stranger to controversy or to the desperate circumstances in which many who were in his care as parish priest and bishop existed. He called his autobiography *Chanctonbury Ring* for that was a place where he *"found a peace I never found in the church"*.

Wilfrid Scawen Blunt claimed that the real spelling was *"Chanclebury Ring."* He gave that as the title of his best known poem without which no Sussex anthology would be complete. That it comes from his *The Love Sonnets of Proteus* (1881) will give a clue to the place of Sussex in his heart.

Wilfrid Scawen Blunt (1840-1922) was a man of Sussex. He was born of a long line of Sussex squires at Petworth house in the days long before the National Trust when it was still a private house. His aunt, his father's sister, was married to George Wyndham, the then owner, who later became the first Lord Leconfield. Sussex was his home throughout his lifetime in spite of absences abroad as a member of the Diplomatic Service and in private travel. And, after a long life, he fulfilled the final words of *Chanclebury Ring* when he was buried in his Arabian travelling blanket in the private woods of his Sussex home not far from Barns Green: the final six lines of the poem are engraved on his tomb.

A many faceted man, he was one of those vividly coloured, larger than life characters that loom out of the Victorian era that would now either be eclipsed by political correctness or celebrated by some sections of the media for other than their real accomplishments. Some call him an amorist: others a philanderer. He was a man who loved and was loved by many women throughout his life but with whom, remarkably, he stayed lifelong friends well after passion was spent.

He left school with ambitions of becoming a poet, ambitions that he was to fulfil throughout a long, eventful and complex life that can be painted here only with the broadest of broad brushes:

> "Say what you will, there is not in the world
> A nobler sight than from this upper Down.
> No rugged landscape here, no beauty hurled
> From its Creator's hand as with a frown;
> But a green plain on which green hills look down
> Trim as a garden plot. No other hue
> Can hence be seen, save here and there the brown
> Of a square fallow, and the horizon's blue.
> Dear checker-work of woods, the Sussex Weald!
> If a name thrills me yet of things on earth,
> That name is thine. How often have I fled,
> To thy Deep hedgerows, and embraced each field,
> Each lag, each pasture,– fields which gave me birth
> And saw my youth, and which must hold me dead."
> Wilfred Scawen Blunt

but a more conventional occupation was considered necessary. In 1859 he entered the Diplomatic Service in which he served for eleven years with postings across Europe and to Buenos Aires. In 1866 whilst posted to Italy he was introduced to Lady Annabella King-Noel whom he was to marry in 1869 and who was to become known as Lady Anne as Blunt's siblings called her. Lady Anne, who was to become a travel writer in her own right, brought with her a distinguished poetic connection. She was the granddaughter of the poet, Lord Byron. She also brought a connection with another kind of writing, the writing of computer programs. Her mother, Byron's daughter, Ada, Countess of Lovelace, otherwise Ada Lovelace (1815-52) was a mathematician. She had been a friend and an assistant to Charles Babbage, the computer pioneer, and she has been credited as amongst the first to write programs for the computer.

Resignation form the Diplomatic Service and changes in circumstances allowed Blunt and Lady Anne to travel widely. This brought Blunt into contact with the people whose causes he was to support and undoubtedly it led to the preservation of the Arab horse.

In April 1873 they left England for Turkey, the first of the eastern travels. In Turkey they wore local dress, travelled on horseback in all weathers and slept on the ground. There they bought Turkeycock, the forerunner of the Crabbet Arabian Stud. He was not pure Arabian blood but the first horse carrying eastern blood that they brought back to England. In following years they travelled widely through Arabia on arduous journeys mounted on horses or camels, sometimes buying horses of the purest Arabian blood that was becoming adulterated though cross breeding even in its native areas. The Crabbet Arabian Stud, founded in 1878 to remedy the breeding defects in Arab horses in Arabia and throughout the world, became world famous. In time, the wheel turned full circle and horses were exported back to reinvigorate the regions from which their blood had originally come.

There were travels both near and far not confined to the home of or the buying of the Arab horse. They fuelled Blunt's anti-imperialism and his support of self determination and home rule for indigenous peoples wherever they might be and whoever the imperialist. After visiting India he was to write, "*Though a good conservative and a member of the Carlton Club, I own to be shocked ... and my faith in British institutions and the blessings of British rule have received a severe blow.*" Of Arabia, "*If I can introduce a pure Arabian breed of horses into England and help to see Arabia free of the Turks I shall not quite have lived in vain.*" Of Africa in the 1880s, "*All that Europe has done by its interference for the last thirty years in Africa has been to introduce fire-arms* (sic)*, drink and syphilis.*"

At first he was reticent but became increasingly open in speech and in print: letters to the newspapers, polemical verse and books. His activities in Ireland led to a short spell of imprisonment that Oscar Wilde thought had an "a*dmirable effect*" on him as a poet but, as an establishment figure, he became increasingly unacceptable to the establishment for his politics that were in advance of his time. He was also accused of gun running in Egypt when the authorities discovered a store of twelve rifles, four revolvers and a small brass cannon. The weapons had been collected for an expedition into the desert that never took place, the cannon being intended as a present for a local ruler. Blunt later recovered the weapons. The cannon still exists. It is of small calibre and, on its carriage, is barely knee height: hardly the stuff of weapons of mass destruction.

Some years before his death Blunt wrote, *"I shall probably be reckoned some day as a poet but not till after I am dead. My politics are too damnable for that."* The poetry was ever there. There were his own books of verse and there were those poets who came to visit. There was Hilaire Belloc, his friend and close neighbour at Shipley. The dying Francis Thompson spent some of his last days in a cottage on Blunt's estate that was lent to him. In 1914, there was the *"Peacock Dinner"* when Blunt was honoured by younger poets at a dinner where a peacock was served. They included Ezra Pound and W B Yeats. John Masefield was supposed to have been there but, in the words of a close observer, *"he is under the thumb of a wife who will not let him go anywhere."*

And others came too. Winston Churchill, also a literary man and a future winner of the Nobel Prize for Literature, was a frequent visitor. Others came to visit Blunt the Arabist who had travelled widely in Arabia, who had studied Islam there, who spoke Arabic and who frequently wore Arab dress at home and in the countryside of Sussex. They included Lawrence of Arabia who told of his adventures and later described Blunt as a *"Prophet."*

It may be, however, that Blunt would best liked to be remembered as a poet but his name is also well remembered in other parts of the world for the causes that he espoused that made his politics apparently so *"damnable"*.

To those who know the geography of Sussex, it may seen strange to continue further southwards with no more word of Hilaire Belloc who lived so long in the village of Shipley not far away. But Belloc was a man who strode literally and metaphorically across Sussex and we will be meeting much more with him further along the Trail.

The southern end of the picturesque, timber-framed house called the Blue Idol is officially the Thakeham Meeting House of the Society of Friends, the Quakers, called so from the guidance of George Fox, the founder of the Society, to his followers that they "*should tremble at the word of the Lord.*" William Penn (1644-1718), the founder of Pennsylvania, helped to found the Thakeham meeting where he worshipped and ministered.

There are many misconceptions about William Penn on both sides of the Atlantic. It is certain that Pennsylvania would not have been founded when and where it was without him: not because he was a benign and peace loving Quaker creating a place of refuge for the oppressed but because, unlike other Quakers, he was a member of the ruling elite with powerful political connections.

Amongst his ideals was that Pennsylvania should, as it did, provide a haven, although at first not totally egalitarian, for the Quakers and others free from persecution. It was also, however, in conception a considerable investment opportunity although, in the event, it proved to be more of a liability than a lucrative asset. There may even be a misconception about the name Pennsylvania. Penn would have preferred it to be called New Wales or, when that was rejected, Sylvania. However his royal patron, the King, insisted that the colony, as it then was, should be named Pennsylvania for Penn's father although Penn feared that it would be thought that the colony was named after himself.

Penn's father, also William, was an admiral under the republican Cromwellian government but successfully transferred his allegiance to the Crown at the Restoration of the Monarchy under Charles II in 1660. He was knighted and achieved power and position. He lent money to the King. He was appointed a Commissioner of the Navy in which capacity he met and became a friend of an Admiralty official, Samuel Pepys. Pepys was to rise to become Secretary to the Admiralty and to be considered as the saviour of the British Navy, as well as leaving a vivid picture of seventeenth century life in his diary. Pepys described his friend, Sir William, as "*a merry fellow and pretty good natured, and sings very loose songs.*" An engaging mental picture comes from the diary when Sir William and Samuel Pepys dug a pit in the garden on the evening of 4th September 1666. There they buried their wine to protect it from the Great Fire of London that was then raging.

Meanwhile, the young Penn was continuing with his education and, although in a position of privilege, was progressing towards becoming a Quaker. In 1660 he entered Oxford University. Tradition has it that the beginnings of his conversion were at Oxford after hearing Thomas Loe, a leading Quaker, preach and that he was expelled in 1662 for attending Quaker meetings. He certainly left the University early and was immediately dispatched abroad by his father. On his return two years later he was still to outward appearances a tall, handsome young man of fashion wearing a sword, a mark of his rank. There had even been a duel when he had been in France. Challenged over some trifling matter by a man with a naked sword in hand, he drew his own and was able to disarm his opponent whose life he spared: such a matter was not worth a man's life. He studied law at Lincoln's Inn in London and then was sent to manage his father's estates in Ireland where he briefly saw military service. He came back in 1667, a Quaker.

The following years saw Penn travelling widely, preaching, ministering and writing much. There were spells of imprisonment for his faith. His social position was no protection from the laws against religious dissent, but it would have given him a close look at the hardships of life far away from his own. He was also petitioning the Crown for the grant to him of a colony in America. There he would be able to ensure liberty of conscience and religious toleration and opportunity.

His first recorded stay in Sussex was in 1672. He moved to live at Warminghurst, about four miles away from the Blue Idol, in 1676. It was to be his home when he was in England for over thirty years and provided a place of stability throughout what proved to be a troublesome period. It was at Warminghurst that in 1681 that he received the charter from King Charles II granting to him the Proprietorship of the colony. Although the Crown's political motives were other than the principles envisaged by Penn, there was nevertheless a giant step forward towards the foundation of a great nation. It was at Warminghurst that the first draft was prepared of the Frame of Government that, after much discussion and amendment, was adopted in 1701 as the Charter of Privileges. That Charter formed the constitution of Pennsylvania. It was from Warminghurst that Penn left for his first visit to Pennsylvania taking with him the draft Frame and many Friends from Sussex to settle the new colony.

Penn's effect on North America was immediate and long lasting even until today. The Charter of Privileges and the principles that it embodied was in due course to have its influence on the Constitution of the United States itself. In Pennsylvania from the start free elections were guaranteed as were jury trials. There was no death penalty except for treason and murder as opposed to England where a death sentence could be imposed for literally hundreds of offences: taxes could only be levied by law: there was religious freedom.

There were enlightened relations with the native Americans governed by the Great Treaty of Shackamaxon that was not broken, at least while Penn was alive. Voltaire, the French philosopher commented that it was the only treaty between those nations, i.e. the North American native peoples, and the Christians which was never sworn to and never broken. The Quakers do not take oaths: the practice is forbidden by Christ (Matthew 5: 34-37). Penn even set a precedent in town planning. The grid pattern in which he laid out the city on Philadelphia became the model for future American cities.

Penn's written output was huge: over one hundred books and pamphlets, mainly on religion and his Christian faith as a Quaker but also on the settlement of Pennsylvania and North American affairs including his Plan for a Union of the Colonies in 1697. His *Some Fruits of Solitude* (1693) remains in print and was much admired by Robert Louis Stevenson who "*found it in all times and places a sweet and peaceful companion.*"

Although the Blue Idol is much as Penn knew it, the great house at Warminghurst is no longer there. It was sold in 1707. The buyer, James Butler, had it pulled down and another built in is place, determined, it is said, "*not to leave a trace of the old Quaker.*" Penn's lasting memorials lie elsewhere starting at the Blue Idol and extending across the Atlantic from there.

NUTBOURNE TO HOUGHTON BRIDGE

From the Rising Sun head south along The Street. Continue past Stream Lane and at Ragman's Castle, where the road swings sharp right, go straight ahead uphill on the private road, which is a public footpath. At the end of this lane, besides Horsecroft Tanners, continue ahead down a narrow passageway. At the stony lane ahead cross straight over to follow a footpath fingerpost into a wood. Keep to the right side of the wood and exit over a small stile into an open field. Three quarters of the way down the field go through a metal gate to your right and continue ahead with the fencing now to your left. Turn right in front of the bungalow and in 30m exit left over a stile onto the public road.

Cross the road here and turn left. In 150m after crossing a small bridge turn right over a stile into a small wood to walk besides the stream. Cross another stile into a more open field and follow the stream round to the right. In 50m cross this stream on a plank bridge and turn left with a large open field now to your right. Cross a substantial wooden bridge over the River Chilt (hence West Chiltington) and smaller plank one to a path, which climbs through the woods to reach a gate onto West Sussex Golf Course.

The West Sussex Golf Club was designed by two golf architects, Guy Campbell and Cecil Hutchinson, and officially opened on St. George's Day 1931. It is an outstanding beautiful heathland course of sand, heather and pine. Sir Peter Allen rates the 6th and 13th at West Sussex as the best inland holes in the British Isles. The Club has a long waiting list for membership.

The path across the course is clearly marked. Take care here and respect those enjoying their golf as you cross the first fairway to the left of the birch tree. Cross the next fairway to the clearly visible gate in the far fence line. Exit through this wooden gate and follow the clear path through the trees. In 250m cross a stile onto a tarmac road and turn left, heading slightly uphill.

In a further 500m walk past the clubhouse and reach a gate onto the private drive to Hurston Place Farm. At the farm go through a large gate and follow the track through the farm buildings down to a second gate and at the T junction ahead turn right to cross a bridge over the River Stor (hence Storrington).

A few metres upstream you can see the remains of a brick wall along the eastern bank with a bridge leading over a side stream to the river. The 1880 map shows a corn mill here and the river, linking as it does with The Arun, may have been used as a small navigation.

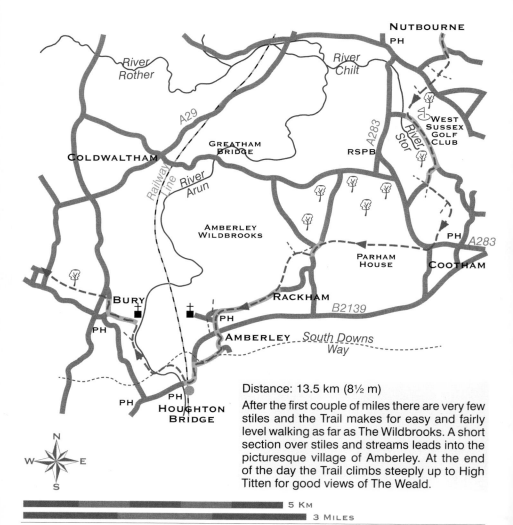

Distance: 13.5 km (8½ m)

After the first couple of miles there are very few stiles and the Trail makes for easy and fairly level walking as far as The Wildbrooks. A short section over stiles and streams leads into the picturesque village of Amberley. At the end of the day the Trail climbs steeply up to High Titten for good views of The Weald.

Follow the tarmac lane as it curves left and begins to climb. After 500m, where the lane swings sharp right, follow a fingerpost indicating a path straight ahead, climbing into the trees. Walk left of the large mound to pass through a wooden gate and then immediately take the left fork heading downhill. At the edge of the wood turn sharp left following an enclosed path between open fields.

Follow the fingerposts around the left hand side of this field and soon reach the mown grass of Parham Airfield. Now keep close to the tree line on your left following the right of way and avoiding any close encounters with tugs or gliders – both of which can appear very quietly and suddenly over the treetops.

This is home to the Southdown Gliding Club, which was formed in 1930. It is one of the oldest, largest and best equipped voluntary clubs in Britain. This location close to the South Downs allows soaring on the up draughts from the Downs. Trial lessons or full one-day courses are available in two- seat trainers; with three tug aircraft and a two-drum winch for launching. The two hundred club members keep over forty privately owned gliders at the airfield.

Before reaching these parked gliders look carefully for a fingerpost on the left leading to a narrow, rough path heading downhill into the trees. There is a precautionary sign just here. The path winds through a small combe with a stream to your left but then soon crosses this on a plank bridge and bears right up the opposite bank. In 50m turn right at a fingerpost to go back down to the stream and cross it again on another plank bridge.

This path leads into a residential close of gnomes. Take the road out of the mobile home park and follow the lane left and right to reach the main A283 near a telephone kiosk. The Crown Inn is just 50m to your left; the Trail, however, continues in the other direction. Cross the road carefully and turn right.

Cootham village hall, on your left, was originally a chapel, built in the 19th century at the instigation of Lord Zouche of Parham House, a travel writer of whom there is mention in the literary section.

In 300m keep left to enter the private drive to Parham Park. The footpath through the park is, of course, always open. Soon pass through the kissing gate besides the lodge to enter the deer park. As the drive crosses the brow of the hill and begins to go left look for a fingerpost showing a path diverging away to the right from the drive towards the trees. Follow this path across open land to reach a metalled drive. Follow the drive straight ahead with views of the house to your left.

Parham House was built in 1577 in classical Elizabethan style. It has expansive gables, tall chimneys, mullioned windows and fine interior panelling. The Great Hall, rising through two storeys, is one of the most magnificent Elizabethan rooms in Britain. The walls are

hung with a splendid collection of 16th century portraits including those of Elizabeth I, who dined here in the 1590s. Rather more recently, in the 1960s, the distinguished theatrical designer Oliver Messel decorated the ceiling of the 160-foot 'Long Gallery'. Around the house stretch 300 acres of ancient deer park and you may be lucky enough to see some of the fallow deer who are descendants of the original herd first recorded in 1628.

Just under 1 km after passing the house, exit through a kissing gate onto the public road and turn left. At the road junction keep left following road signs to Amberley and in 200m at the Old School House turn right in front of the building

with a sandstone outcrop to your right. Follow the broad path ahead besides the wooden fence with woodland to your right and more open land to the left. Go past Pine Cottage and at the footbridge over the small stream turn left with a view of the 'Wildbrooks' now to your right.

The Wildbrooks are more correctly 'Weald Brooks' This natural area of wetland was the scene of a famous victory when it was the first site ever to be saved from agricultural drainage because of its wildlife.

A coalition of local people, the Sussex Wildlife Trust and RSPB fought and won a landmark public inquiry in the early 1970s and now over half of all the British aquatic plant species are found here. The brooks regularly flood in winter and become home to hundreds of wigeon, pintail, teal & mallard as well as large numbers of Bewick's swans. The outstandingly rich ditches are full of flowering plants and all sorts of rare insects and other invertebrates including the hairy dragonfly and water scorpion. And in the centre Amberley Swamp is a particularly special, mysteriously wild place, with a strange quality. An 82-hectare area in the western section is now managed jointly by the Sussex Wildlife Trust and the RSPB.

In 150m cross a stile up onto a mound and turn half right to pass between the old mill on the right and the house to your left. Cross a stile into the woods and follow the narrow path to cross plank bridges and stiles into a sometimes waterlogged meadow. Cross the lower part of the meadow to a bridge over a small watercourse. Go through a hedge to face a long straight path heading uphill across the middle of an open field. On reaching the public road turn right and follow this for exactly one mile (1609m) to reach the Black Horse Inn at Amberley.

Bob Copper expressed his love of this village with the words:
"At Amberley the days are free, The skylark tops the Mount so bare,
But cannot fly near half so high, As soars my heart when I am there."

Amberley is known as the Pearl of Sussex. It has been sketched, painted and written about for hundreds of years and is truly picturesque – although perhaps in a slightly self-conscious way. It is always a delight to wander through its quiet lanes and visit the church, the pottery, the village shop and the pub – and maybe even the luxury of Amberley Castle Hotel for afternoon tea.

For a closer look at the village continue straight ahead into Hog Lane and follow it slowly around to reach Church Street. A right turn at the T-junction will lead to St. Michael's Church. From here retrace your steps all the way along Church Street to the 'village square' and turn right to the B2139.

Turn left at the Black Horse and walk down past the village stores to the busy B2139. Cross carefully and walk up into Mill Lane.

As you climb this rather steep hill think back to just 100 years ago when Mr. E.C. Gordon England came up here on 27th June 1909 with the sole purpose of jumping off the top! That day, in 'The Albatross', the 16 year old set the world record for 'a glide' at 58 seconds – a feat that was not surpassed until the Wright Brothers resumed gilding at Kitty Hawk some years later. Gordon wrote at the time: "The wind was just right and the machine – which was in charge of me, not I of it – headed out over the valley to a ploughed field where it landed gently".

At the top of this hill join the South Downs Way National Trail and turn right to follow the tarmac road towards Houghton Bridge. At the bottom of this lane, known as 'High Titten', cross the main road carefully and turn left following the path inside the hedge to pass by the Chalk Pits Museum entrance and walk under the railway bridge. Here there are the facilities of a pub, a tearoom, a restaurant and a railway station.

George and Dragon, Houghton

And busy as it may seem today, this spot has seen much more activity in its long history. In the summer of 1895 special trains were laid on from Victoria Station, some with as many as 19 coaches, to transport over 1,000 anglers here from the metropolis to enjoy a day's competitive fishing for the famous 'Amberley trout'. This was traditionally one of the seven 'Good Things of Sussex' – the others being Chichester lobster, Pulborough eel, Selsey cockle, Arundel mullet, Rye herring and the Bourne wheatear – huge numbers of which were trapped for food until the 20th century!

To the Arun

A world where the population, save for a few, had been blinded was becoming dominated by the triffids: the homicidal, mobile, oil producing plants described in John Wyndhams's novel, *The Day of the Triffids*.

They had broken free of their chains and were roaming town and country. Bill Masen briefly meets Josella Playton and then becomes separated from her in the increasing anarchy and desolation of London. He sets out in search of her on a trail that leads to a dead end. But he remembers that when they had spoken of where it might be safe for them to go she mentioned the Sussex Downs and "... *a lovely old farmhouse on the north side, looking towards Pulborough. It's not on the top of the hills but it's well up the side.*" He also remembers that the house stood on the north side of the hills and had an impression that, "*it faced across the, low, marshy country that separated them from Pulborough.*"

He makes his way through devastation populated by marauding triffids to Pulborough, a village a mile due west of Nutbourne, that looks across Amberley Wild Brooks straight to the Downs and the Arun Gap. There, with a spotlight found in the village, he signals in hope towards the Downs.

But where is the farmhouse? From the descriptions in the book it must be on the shoulder of Amberley Mount. The route of the Trail does not give the view from Pulborough but, later, south of Amberley, it climbs Mill Lane up the face of the Downs towards the site.

South of Nutbourne the Trail runs along the edge of Parham Airfield before meeting a main road, the A283, where it turns right towards Parham Park and Parham House. A left turn would lead into Storrington, one of the places where the tormented soul of Francis Thompson (1859-1907) fled from *The Hound of Heaven* and where it may have caught him.

Francis Thompson who from his appearance, in the words of E V Lucas, "*would be taken for a poet even by the least discriminating observer*" was born in Preston in Lancashire. The son of a doctor it was intended that he should follow in that profession. He failed his final examinations three times. He also became addicted to laudanum, a derivative of opium. In 1885 he left home for London to try to fulfil an ambition to become a poet. He existed there for three years homeless, destitute and drug addicted, but still managing to write, until his work was recognized by Wilfrid Meynell, the editor of a magazine, who started to publish his poetry. He was literally rescued by Wilfrid Meynell and his wife, Alice, who opened their home to him and through whom he was for a while able to find sanctuary with the White Canons at their monastery in Storrington which is still there. As we have already heard, Wilfrid Scawen Blunt provided a home for him in some of the last days of his life before he returned to London, where he died of tuberculosis.

He has been suspected of being Jack the Ripper, presumably fuelled by his medical knowledge and his experience of the lower side of London life. But the last words should rest with E V Lucas; "*He never said an unworthy thing, he never wrote a commonplace line*".

A plaque beside the drive to Parham is a reminder of the many and varied occupants of the present house since its foundation stone was laid in 1577. These include the already mentioned Robert Curzon, 14th Baron Zouche of Harringworth (1810-73): traveller, diplomat, collector of manuscripts and scholar.

His travels in the Near East and Egypt, to Mount Athos in Greece and to Italy led to a collection of intellectually valuable manuscripts that he purchased and three books: *Visit to the Monasteries of the Levant* (1849) on his search for manuscripts that proved sufficiently popular to run into a number of editions, *An Account of the most Celebrated Libraries of Italy* (1854) and *Armenia* (1854). As a diplomat he served in Constantinople, as Istanbul then was, where he continued his search for manuscripts and where he was appointed a commissioner for setting the boundaries between Persia and Turkey, for which he was decorated by both heads of state. His interest in manuscripts was not only in what was written but, as a student of handwriting, in how it was written. It was his intention to use his collection for a treatise on the history of handwriting. This was never completed. He was criticised for not allowing the manuscripts to remain where he found them but much would have perished if he had done so.

In an unpublished paper Kim Leslie draws attention to the extraordinary richness of the literary connections of the area immediately around Amberley. In the 1904 first edition of his *Highways & Byways in Sussex*, E V Lucas, described the then very rural village of Amberley as, "*a huge stockyard, smelling of straw and cattle*" but "*It is sheer Sussex – chalky soil, whitewashed cottages, huge wagons.*" The cattle and the wagons had gone from the book by the time of the second edition

in 1935 although cows did continue to come into the village twice a day to be milked until the 1950s. In 1935 Amberley remained "*sheer Sussex*" and to the "*chalky soil*" and "*whitewashed cottages*" there were added "*thatched roofs*" and "*flowery gardens.*" And so it is today.

It was the Meynells who helped to emphasize the Amberley area as a literary centre of the twentieth century. Alice (1847-1922), a distinguished poet, essayist, editor and women's suffragist, although she disapproved of militant action, was better known to the public than her husband. The ubiquitous E V Lucas reported that Thomas Hardy thought that she should be appointed Poet Laureate on the death of Alfred Austin in 1913, "*not only for her distinction, but because there was no reason why a woman should make a worse Laureate than a man.*" Robert Bridges was appointed instead. Lucas felt that she would, perhaps, have done as little to produce official poems as Bridges but that she would not have been so forthright to say as he did, "*I'll see them damned first.*"

Having lived long in London the Meynells settled in Greatham on the banks of the Arun barely two miles north of Amberley as the crow flies: or three as the course of the river runs in curves along the edge of the Wild Brooks. There, to the Meynells, surrounded by their children and their children's families housed in cottages about the estate, came leading literary figures and intellectuals of the day. We have already heard of Francis Thompson who walked the Downs above Storrington and like so many before and since found peace, consolation and inspiration. Others included Edward Thomas and D H Lawrence both of whom also walked on the Downs. On his visit in 1915 Lawrence accompanied Eleanor Farjeon on a walk to Chichester twenty miles away over the Downs.

They met early *"in one of those white Sussex mists which muffle the meadows before sunrise, lying breast-high on the earth, her last dream before waking."* He found that she walked too fast for him and told her, *"I must teach you to walk like a tramp. When you are to walk all day you must learn to amble and rest every mile or so."* They padded on gently. The sun melted the mists. They *"sang scraps of songs, and every two miles lolled on the grass."* They found Stane Street, the old Roman Road across the Downs to Chichester, and then lost themselves. They found themselves again and the Literary Trail will catch up with them further on.

The name of Eleanor Farjeon (1881-1965), poet, lyricist, novelist, playwright, biographer, story maker and story teller and, especially, friend and comforter, is not as well known as it once was but it is certain that most, if not all, will be familiar with one of her works. In 1923 she was commissioned to write three hymns for a total fee of nine guineas. Nearly fifty years later, and after her death so that she was not able to benefit personally, the words of one of these, *Morning has Broken*, was taken into the popular music hit parade by the singer then known as Cat Stevens.

She grew up in a house full of books, some eight thousand of them, with talented, literary and artistic parents and siblings and she started writing from an early age. Her father was a popular Victorian novelist: her mother the descendant of a line of four generations of American actors the first of which had emigrated to America in the days of David Garrick in the 18th century. When young she was painfully shy in public and much under the influence of her father and elder brother. Her father died in 1903 leaving his family in comparative poverty. It became necessary for her to earn a living from her writing.

She met and fell for Edward Thomas in 1912 although it was only friendship on his part. It was she and Robert Frost who set Edward Thomas to writing the poetry that they could see in his prose. His first poem was written in 1914 and the whole of his verse was confined to the last years of his life until he was killed in France in 1917, another poet consumed in the waste of war.

It was in 1913 that she made her first visit to the Meynells at Greatham and in 1917 she took a cottage close to Amberley: The End Cottage, Mucky Lane, Houghton. Here she lived alone for nearly two years that she thought may have been the most important years of her life bringing her away from fears and humiliations that had been with her since childhood. Her best known book and that which established her reputation, *Martin Pippin in the Apple Orchard*, comes from this time. Although she did write for children and this book is now thought of as a children's book, it was not written as such. It is a whimsical fantasy that was sent in instalments to Captain Victor Hallam who was serving in the War in France: a complete contrast to the grimness of war. It is set near the village of Adversane a mile or so to the south of Billingshurst. Like Edward Thomas she was fascinated by the romance of old Sussex place names. Adversane seemed to her to have come from the world of medieval romance and the troubadours of that age.

From Houghton she went back to London although she was to return to visit Greatham and the Meynells in later years. In all she wrote some 99 books and musical works. She was honoured for her work. In 1956 she received both the Library Association's Carnegie medal and the first award of the International Hans Christian Andersen medal for *The Little Bookroom*. In 1959 she was awarded the American Regina medal for her work for children. It is reported that she declined becoming a Dame of the British Empire as she did "*not wish to become different from the milkman.*" After her death the Children's Book Circle created the annual Eleanor Farjeon Award for distinguished contribution to children's books.

Of the Downs she wrote, "*They've healed me more, and given me more strength and certainty and peace than any other living thing.*"

Eleanor Farjeon is not Amberley's only connection to children's literature. Noel Streatfield (1895-1986) was born in Amberley, one of the daughters of the vicar. She wrote for both children and adults but her most popular book is *Ballet Shoes* (1936) which is still in print. A ballet and a film have both been based on it. She was able to draw on her own ten years experience as a not entirely successful actress following World War 1 during which she had worked in a munitions factory.

Nor should the illustrators be forgotten. The last home of Cicely Mary Baker (1895-1973) was in Amberley. She originated the *Flower Fairy* series of books that are still going strong over 70 years since their first appearance in 1923. There was Arthur Rackham (1867-1939) too. From 1920 to 1930 he lived and worked at Houghton House. He is buried in Amberley churchyard where he and his wife are also commemorated by a memorial plaque on the churchyard wall. His style is unmistakable. Although predating Tolkien, Rackham's gnarled trees

and twisting roots sheltering strange beings can call to mind Tolkien's dark and mysterious woodlands. His best known work was for *Fairy Tales of the Brothers Grimm* (1900). Later work includes Poe's *Tales of Mystery and Imagination* in 1935. He had been asked to illustrate the first edition of *Wind in the Willows* in 1908 but to his regret was not able to accept the commission. The last works that he completed just before his death, however, were illustrations for an edition of *Wind in the Willows* that was first published in 1940.

Arnold Bennett (1867-1931) came to Amberley in 1926 He rented the house now called Boxwood that is in Church Street. It was a stay of only eight weeks from 21st May, but it was at a significant point in his personal life. He was a well established and successful novelist; a rich man from his books, he was also a playwright and the highest paid literary journalist of the day. He had separated from his wife Marguerite in 1921 but had not pursued a divorce, although he had grounds to do so. He did not wish to attract the glare of publicity that the case would bring in a time when divorce was far less common. He also considered that once married, it was for life. In 1922, however, he met an actress, Dorothy Cheston, who was appearing in one of his plays. Their daughter Virginia was born 13th April 1926. Bennett was reconsidering the question of a divorce but it was at Amberley that he recorded in his diary on 25th May, "*I heard definitely from Marguerite that she would not agree to a divorce.*" Bennett and Dorothy stayed together until his death five years later.

While at Amberley he completed his novel *The Strange Vanguard*. He estimated that two thirds of it had been written at Amberley and that he had "*never worked more easily.*" He did, however, find time for walking and visitors who included H G Wells, Aldous and Julian Huxley, and John Cowper Powys who was within walking distance at Burpham. Amberley, called "*Cander*", and its surroundings feature in his short story *The Woman Who Stole Everything* that he wrote soon after his visit to the village.

Bennett was born at Hanley, one of the Five Towns that formed the English Potteries, the home of such names of Wedgwood, Spode, Minton and Coalport. The son of a self-educated solicitor it was intended that he too should follow his father's profession. His own ambition was to write and, borrowing the train fare from his mother, he went to London where after a spell in a clerical position with a firm of solicitors he was able to turn to writing full time both as novelist and journalist being, for a time, the editor of the weekly periodical *Woman*. But the Potteries never left him. In restaurants or other peoples' houses he would look at the makers' marks under the plates to see at which factory in the Five Towns they had been made.

The Becketts also passed through Amberley in their search for the crock of gold. They discovered "*Golden Meadows*" that are fairy fields from a million buttercups which some believe are the root of Amberley's name.

But the Trail must move on to the Bridge Inn at Houghton Bridge. Here Belloc's *The Four Men* waited out the rain on their way to Harting which was the end of their trail "*where the county ends and where you come to shapeless things.*" As they waited they told of their first loves and not entirely with regard for the truth.

HOUGHTON BRIDGE TO DUNCTON

Immediately under the bridge turn right following the footpath fingerpost down a gravel drive to a stile. The path now leads behind the mobile homes to the eastern bank of the River Arun. Turn right to walk along the riverside and cross a stile to rejoin the South Downs Way. In 300m at the large footbridge, cross the river and turn right following the raised bank as it swings right to head north. Stay on the bank for 1km, passing through two kissing gates and finally cross two stiles over locked gates besides River House to reach a bench and a directional post.

© Stephen Cobb

This was the site of the ferry to Amberley – operated for many years by Mrs Marshall and her mother in the early 1900s (as shown in the sketch) and latterly by Bob Dudden until1955 when the ferry closed. In the Parish Council minutes of the 1890's it is frequently written that "the question of the bell at the ferry was postponed until the next meeting." One wonders what on earth that difficult question might have been! From the opposite side of the river it is now a 2½ km walk to Bury. There is a delightful account in the literary section of Bob Copper's encounter here.

Turn left away from the river towards Bury Church. In just a few metres turn right besides Manor Cottage to enter the churchyard up a flight of steep steps.

There are three bells hanging in the church tower. The earliest, from around 1400, is inscribed 'Sancte Dunstane ora pro nobis' (St. Dunstan pray for us) and a later one of 1599 has 'God save the Queen' – Elizabeth I, of course.

Having visited this lovely church leave by the western gate onto a raised footpath

Mystery of ferrywoman sketch

and continue up the lane through the village to reach the crossroads. A short distance ahead lies Bury House, where a blue plaque commemorates John Galsworthy. To continue on the Trail turn north from the crossroads, uphill along The Street towards Bury Hollow and in 300m, at the top of the rise, fork left between Street Cottage and Kesters Cottage on a broad drive heading slightly uphill. This soon narrows to a path going downhill to meet the very busy A29.

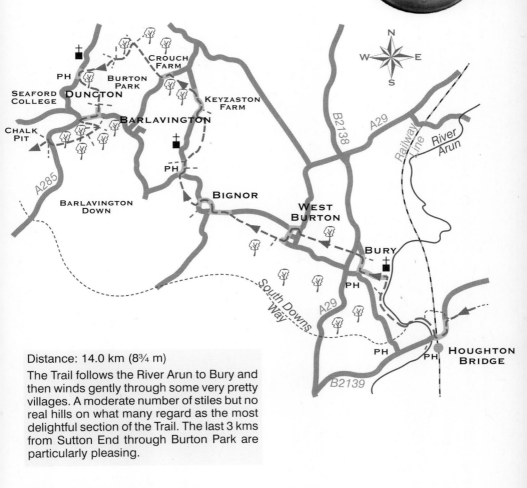

Distance: 14.0 km (8¾ m)

The Trail follows the River Arun to Bury and then winds gently through some very pretty villages. A moderate number of stiles but no real hills on what many regard as the most delightful section of the Trail. The last 3 kms from Sutton End through Burton Park are particularly pleasing.

5 KM

3 MILES

Cross carefully to the flint cottage opposite besides Hillside Nurseries. Pass to the left of the cottage and then turn right following the footpath fingerpost. Continue ahead over a stile between two gates and follow the hedgeline on your left for 100m to reach a second stile into a very narrow path, which slopes awkwardly.

As you approach the trees look carefully to your right down the bank and you may spot a commemorative stone to Fred Hughes and his wife. Fred "Worked these fields and loved them. He built the farm you see and never wanted any more – only to be free." The words added later about Winifred are even more poignant. Take a look and then rest awhile on the nearby seat provided by their children; and reflect for a moment.

The Trail drops down a hill (in spring covered in wild garlic) to two stiles leading onto a plank bridge. Turn half right to the metal gate in the far corner of the next field. Cross a stile besides the gate and follow the hedgeline and ditch on your right heading slightly uphill. Just before the top of this field turn right across a stile and continue now keeping the hedgeline to your left. In 300m, near the top left corner of the field, look for a metal gate to your left and follow the yellow arrow into a sunken path heading slightly uphill. This track broadens into a drive and soon reaches the public road. This is the village of West Burton.

The large stone house a little way down to the left is Cooke's house, (formerly Coke's) one of the oldest in West Burton. It was originally a manor and is named after one of the early owners, Richard Coke, who lived here in the 1580s. The splendid Jacobean gateway is protected by the spreading cedar – surely one of the most beautiful trees in Sussex.

Our Trail goes in the other direction, to the right, and then immediately left following signs to Bignor, Sutton & Roman Villa. At the next road junction turn left again to follow the minor road downhill. At the bottom of the hill on reaching a T-junction, turn right and in 200m reach Fogdens.

Look carefully and you will see a scallop shell set into the side of the small bridge over the stream. In medieval times the scallop shell became the badge of pilgrims to the shrine of St James at Santiago de Compostela, in Galicia, northwest Spain.

To this day it remains the symbol of the Camino de Santiago and marks many of the pilgrim trails. Because these shells are native to the shores of Galicia, they also functioned as proof of completion – and they happen to be just the right size for gathering water to drink or eating from as a makeshift bowl. Because they were seen as two unique halves, which could not be joined to any other, scallop shells have also been used as symbols of fidelity, both in marriage and in political partnerships and that may be a more logical explanation for this one.

Keep to the right of the timber-framed house and walk with the stream on your left. Cross two plank bridges through this pleasant watercourse past the site of an old Mill Pond and eventually emerge into a large open field with views of the Downs ahead. Turn right and walk along the edge of the field, with the large hedge to your right, for 300m. In the corner of the field turn right on a wooden footbridge over a stream into another large field. Immediately cross a plank bridge and head just to the left of the white cottage in the distance. On reaching the public road turn left. (Note – if this path is 'cropped out' it may be necessary to walk around the left hand edge of this large field to reach the same exit onto the road).

The Roman Villa is just a few metres to your right. It was discovered in July 1811 when George Tupper, whilst ploughing his father's field, struck a large stone believed to have been the piscina in the Ganymede Room. Like most of our Roman sites, it evolved over several centuries, starting life as a simple farmstead around AD190 just west of the Roman road from Chichester to London.

Over the centuries it developed into a palatial governor's house with 65 rooms forming a complete square around a central courtyard, with another nine farm outbuildings, rather unusually, outside the main complex. The location of these farm buildings suggests that it may have been a very large farming estate of perhaps 2,000 acres.

The north corridor mosaic, which extends some 24m, is the longest on display in this country and, of the many other beautiful mosaics on display, one of the finest is that of Ganymede being carried by an eagle from Mount Ida. A mosaic about the size of a modern living room, 5m by 3m, would need more than 120,000 separate pieces of tile for its completion. Mistakes in the completion of the design were, therefore, not uncommon! The villa is open to the public from March to the end of October.

© Terry Owen

At the road junction ahead, on the edge of Bignor, turn right following the road sign to Sutton & Duncton. The road passes the beautiful old Yeoman's House and bends left to reach the church. Turn left at the church going quite steeply downhill. On passing 'Charmans', half way down the hill, turn right through a wooden gate and follow the footpath down a grassy bank.

Numerous streams flow northwards from springs at the foot of the chalk escarpment of the South Downs. These streams usually flow in steep, narrow valleys, such as the one here, and many were artificially dammed to form millponds or ornamental water features. This widespread availability of water from springs and local wells gave rise to many of the pretty downland villages through which the Trail passes. Much of the villages' attractive, unpretentious character comes from the variety of building materials used: there is a mixture of flint, brick, sandstone, rendering and half-timber. Local rock, known as 'clunch', with a washed out, whitish colour is also widely used.

Cross a narrow plank bridge and follow the stream through this sometimes-waterlogged valley to reach a second, substantial plank bridge besides an attractive pond with the converted mill house on the far side. Cross another stream to a narrow stile (beware of barbed wire!) into a grassy field and walk uphill towards the hedge on the skyline. At the top of the rise cross a stile and a step and continue ahead on a well-defined track across the middle of the open field. At the far side follow the track straight ahead between the houses to emerge at the White Horse, Sutton.

The White Horse Inn has a mellow exterior, hidden for much of the year by Virginia Creeper. For two and a half centuries this has been the village alehouse and the vaulted ceiling of the dining room shows this was once the beer cellar. In the late 1980s Albert Roux came to live at Sutton End and once every month he or Michel cooked dinner at the White Horse. Perhaps the very first 'gastropub' in England.

Continue northwards along the Petworth road with the pub to your left. Pass the village hall and telephone kiosk (ignoring a path here) and as Sutton church comes clearly into view turn right in front of Old School House. Follow the surfaced road downhill and take the left fork onto a grassy track leading to a stile. The path through the bushes soon emerges into an open field with good views to the north of Petworth and the greensand ridge. Continue down the right side of the field to cross a stile into a larger open field. Walk around the left edge of this field to a fingerpost at the bottom of the tree line and walk past it to a second post with yellow footpath arrows. Here turn half left into the corner of the field. Cross the stile and follow a wire fence on your right to reach a plank bridge and stile. Cross the middle of the next grazing field towards a delightful thatched cottage where three further stiles lead behind the building onto the public road. Turn right along the road for 200m and walk past the entrance to the strangely named 'Keyzaston' on your right.

Keep to the right hand side of the road as it dips down to pass The Old Poor House and then cross a small stream. In a further 125m turn left following a tarmac drive going uphill past the sign for Sutton End house. At the top of the rise where the drive turns sharp left into the house continue straight ahead on a broad, somewhat sandy track further into the woods. Follow this pleasant track for 400m and eventually enter a 'holly tunnel' going downhill to meet a public road. Turn left and follow the lane for 200m to the top of the rise. The road turns left with Crouch Farm to the right.

This is the centre of Barlavington Farms, organic milk producers. The milk is sold to OMSCo, which was formed in 1994 by a group of farming operations in the West of England, including The Prince of Wales' Duchy of Cornwall Home Farm. The members now number well over 300 farmers, and they supply the majority of organic milk produced in this country.

Here look for a fingerpost indicating a broad track straight ahead. Walk past the delightful cottage to your right and cross two stiles besides metal gates to walk straight ahead on a broad track heading downhill.

This track passes clear evidence of the Greensand Ridge, which we last saw at Nutbourne. Follow it straight ahead to reach the southern banks of Chingford Pond.

This is one of two hammer ponds built in the 16th century to power the most southerly iron works in West Sussex, situated about 300m north of here. There is now a water mill there, built in 1784 on the site of the former ironworks. The whole area is a designated nature reserve. Waterfowl can be seen all year round and there is a rich variety of summer dragonflies – such as the scarce Chaser and Emperor species.

Passing the beautiful lake to your left you soon cross the watercourse feeding the third pond and reach a wooden gate. Continue ahead through the gate following the track slightly uphill. Soon reach a gravelled drive and follow it straight ahead through a small housing development whose grounds have been tastefully and expensively landscaped.

These give the appearance of being well-established dwellings but most were in fact only constructed in the late 1990s following the closure of St. Michael's School at Burton House in 1994.

After passing 'Chestnut House' on your left the drive swings left where there is a path through a gate to the right and a path straight ahead over a stile. Here follow the drive to the left, passing on the corner the most magnificent sweet chestnut tree in Sussex – planted in the 1700s and still going strong. The drive reaches the buildings of the converted Burton House and swings right then left to the gate of the tiny church.

Burton Church dates at least from 1075 – with some speculation that it may well have earlier Saxon origins – and is one of the smallest churches in Sussex. Its chancel measures just 3.75m by 3.5m. The original dedication has long been lost but in 2003 it was named after St Richard of Chichester to mark the 750th anniversary of his death.

There are many monuments to the Goring family and their descendants, who lived at Burton House for well over 300 years. But one of the most unusual features is the remarkable early 16th cent wall painting of a young woman tied head downwards on a cross. She has a mass of deep red hair and many believe her to be St. Wilgeforte, one of the nine daughters of the King of Portugal. She had vowed to remain chaste, but her pagan father had other plans, and arranged to marry her off against her will. She prayed that she might become so ugly that her suitor would cancel their union. She miraculously grew a full beard and moustache (successfully repelling the suitor) and devoted the rest of her life to God. However, the rest of her life was fairly short, since her father was so furious that he had her crucified!

From the church gate continue to follow the drive southwards for just 60m, At the second fingerpost take the footpath going off at a slight angle to the right into an enclosed path between two wire fences and diverging slowly away from the drive.

In 400m cross a stile and plank bridge and walk onto the tarmac drive. Turn right and follow the wide drive for 5 minutes to reach the busy A285. Turn left and keep to the left hand side of the road to the Cricketers Inn at Duncton.

The inn was built in the 16th century and was originally called The Swan. However, on his retirement, the well-known Sussex cricketer James Dean acquired the lease and re-named it The Cricketers in honour of his friends and drinking partners. He was born in Duncton in 1816 and his nickname was "Joyous Jem." He was a celebrated all-rounder who played 112 times for Sussex between 1835 and 1860. Over the Christmas holiday of 1881 he invited his friend John Wisden (founder of the cricketing almanac) to be his houseguest at The Cricketers. They spent a most enjoyable Christmas Eve together but sadly the next morning Dean was found to have died in his sleep. The inn sign shows images of 'Jem' on one side and the perhaps better known 'W.G. Grace' on the other.

In 150m, before the pub, reach Dye House Lane on your left and turn left following the bridleway signs

Across the Arun and Under the Downs

To some *The Four Men* published in 1911 is Hilaire Belloc's masterpiece. Belloc called it a farrago – "*a disordered mixture: a confused mass of objects or people*" (*The Chambers Dictionary* 9th ed.). It tells the story of a walk, and Belloc was a great walker, across Sussex, both East and West.

On 29th October 1902 Belloc was sitting in 'The George' at Robertsbridge almost on the border of Sussex with Kent. He was "*drinking that port of theirs and staring at the fire*" and he determined to journey across Sussex to his home country. He and Grizzlebeard, who appeared whilst Belloc was in his reverie, set out next day. Before they had gone far they met the Sailor and the Poet and the four travelled on together. As they went they talked and argued, sang, declaimed poetry and made up more, visiting many a convenient inn en route.

They reached the Bridge Inn at Houghton Bridge during the course of 1st November 1902 on their journey westward. For a while, the Trail shadows their route beneath the line of the Downs by Bury and Westburton and Sutton to Duncton where the Trail and *The Four Men* part company. The Trail turns to climb the Downs whilst *The Four Men* stopped at 'The Cricketers' before continuing their journey. The Trail can only shadow *The Four Men* for they walked mainly along roads that in 1902 were unmade and largely free from the traffic that overpopulates them today to the discomfort and danger of those who would walk.

At the start of the journey from the Bridge Inn there is a slight divergence. The Trail follows the course of the Arun upstream to Bury but *The Four Men* crossed the bridge and went up the hill, past where Eleanor Farjeon and Arthur Rackham were to live in their turn, to the "St George and the Dragon" (sic), another of those still practising inns, before themselves turning towards Bury. It is not recorded whether they stopped at the inn but the distance may have been too short even for their curiosity.

If one turns downstream along the course of the Arun as it reaches towards the sea, making sure that one is on the east side, or crosses to that side at South Stoke, one passes below Burpham and more testimony to the literary fertility of the area.

Edward Lear (1812-1888) stayed often at Peppering close to Burpham. He was a respected zoological and landscape artist who travelled widely publishing accounts of his travels that he illustrated himself but he is best remembered for his nonsense verse and for popularizing the limerick. It does not appear that he wrote a limerick that involved any inhabitant of Burpham.

"There was an old person of Shoreham,
Whose habits were marked by decorum;
He bought an umbrella and sat in the cellar,
Which pleased all the people of Shoreham."

Shoreham seems to be the closest that he came.

Hilaire Belloc, in one of his many facets, succeeded him in the world of nonsense and was considered to be equal to Lewis Carroll and superior to Lear. Belloc is known to some only as a writer of comic verse his other work overshadowed by *The Bad Child's Book of Beasts* (1896), *Cautionary Tales for Children* (1907) and their like.

Tansy (1914)

Tickner Edwardes (1865-1944), the bee-man of Burpham, first came to Burpham as a young man. He was another who did not want to follow in the footsteps of his father's career. Instead he became a journalist and bee keeper, his first and most popular books being on bee keeping: *The Bee Master of Warrilow* (1906) and *The Lore of the Honey Bee* (1908). At the suggestion of his publishers he wrote a novel based on bee keeping. This, and those that followed, were never wholly successful although his most popular, *Tansy* (1914), was filmed on the Downs behind Burpham in 1921 and starred Alma Taylor. Although nearly fifty, he enlisted in the army at the outbreak of the First World War in 1914. His wartime experiences led him to train for Holy Orders when the War was over. He was ordained in 1920 and, after service in parishes elsewhere, he returned to Burpham as its vicar in 1927. He resigned the living in 1935 but remained in Burpham, still writing, for the rest of his life. He is buried in the churchyard.

There was another literary bee keeper on the Downs. Sherlock Holmes retired to a small farm on the South Downs among his bees and his books where he too wrote on bee keeping: the *Practical Handbook of Bee Culture, with some Observations upon the Segregation of the Queen.* But that was much further to the east.

John Cowper Powys (1872-1963) was one of a trio of talented brothers all of whom were published authors. He came to Sussex as a young man in 1893 to teach in Hove. He moved to Burpham in 1902 where he much valued his privacy erecting signs "*Trespassers will be Prosecuted*" on boundaries of his property particularly to deter children from playing to his disturbance. The playing continued but the signs did not, ending in the ditch. His best known books are set in the West Country: *A Glastonbury Romance* (1932), *Weymouth Sands* (1934) and *Maiden Castle* (1940). *After My Fashion,* that he started in 1919 but was published posthumously in 1980 is set in Sussex including scenes in a village reminiscent of Burpham. He spent much of his later years in America eventually retiring to Wales.

Another who came to the village and did not leave it being buried in the churchyard is Mervyn Peake (1911-1968). He gazed across the Arun Valley to Arundel dominated by its castle and received inspiration for Gormenghast and his trilogy of richly gothic novels featuring Titus, 77th earl of Groan. Peake was also a poet and an artist. Amongst other works he illustrated *The Rime of the Ancient Mariner* (1943) and *Treasure Island* (1949). He also followed the local tradition for nonsense with *A Book of Nonsense* (1972).

We have, however, diverted from the Trail and need to follow the direction of *The Four Men* which is what the late Bob Copper OBE (1915-2005), to whom *The Four Men* was 'the book', did in the early 1990s.

Keith with Bob Copper

The Copper family through several generations, but perhaps most with Bob Copper, are known world wide for the preservation and development of song: one hesitates to use the expression 'folk song'. That may conjure a particular image that is far removed from the reality of the Coppers' musical roots deep seated in the English countryside; beards and ethnic sweaters are not part of the Coppers' essential equipment.

But Bob Copper's writings also deserve attention especially in any consideration of Sussex literature. His books *A Song for Every Season* (1971), *Songs & Southern Breezes* (1973) and *Early to Rise* (1976) are mainly centred in East Sussex in and about Rottingdean where the Coppers have lived and worked on the land for centuries. His words commemorate, if not celebrate, a way of life that in reality was not part of some vanished golden age and was nothing less than hard, certainly by today's standards. It had been passing with increased speed during his lifetime: a way of life unknown and alien to those born only a few generations later but the values and strengths, humour and understandings of which would not be anywhere misplaced. In his book, *Across Sussex With Belloc* (1994), Bob traced the way of *The Four Men*. For a short stretch Bob's path and the Literary Trail coincide as both approach the village of Bury where Bob tells the story of years before when Bury had been served by a ferry and he and his wife had approached Bury from the opposite bank.

Bob Dudden had become the ferryman in 1927 the year after Arnold Bennett had crossed to the river to Bury by the ferry. On 25th May 1926, the same day that he heard that his wife would not agree to a divorce, he went walking from Amberley: "*Suddenly I came to the hidden river Arun & no bridge.*" He was ferried across but learnt at Bury Church that it was three miles back to Amberley unless he went back by the ferry. He would not do that and walked back the long way. He got back "*tired but in much better breath*" having picked up some ideas for his novel en route.

CHURCH AND RIVER FERRY CLOSED

Bob Dudden retired in the mid 1950s and the ferry ceased to run soon afterwards.

"I remember the river at Bury where we shouted across to old Bob Dudden, the ferryman, who was sawing logs in the garden of his cottage on the opposite side. But we shouted in vain until at last the log dropped to the ground. Then, straightening his back and lighting his pipe, all the while effecting not to have heard our call, he presently looked up with feigned surprise, walked leisurely to the wooden steps on his side of the water, untied the painter of his punt and slowly paddled across to pick us up. It was all a charade, but it was played out with such good-humoured grace, and it carried such a salutary lesson for anyone more accustomed to the headlong rush of urban life, that the fare of two old-fashioned brown pennies he diffidently asked for seemed painfully inadequate. Yet he resolutely refused to take more, thereby driving home another lesson. To meet a man like Bob the Ferryman was an edifying experience. In the course of less than ten minutes, in his quiet, unhurried way, he had firmly knocked on the head two of the commonest of human weaknesses — impatience and avarice."

Later in the same year that Bennett took his walk, but after he had left Amberley for good, John Galsworthy (1867-1933) came to live at the stone Tudor style mansion that had been built in 1910, Bury House. He was house hunting but viewed Bury House on impulse. With its fifteen bedrooms, it was not what he was looking for. Although he could easily afford it, it was outside the budget that he had set for himself. It was the view of the Downs as he went round the side of the house that sold it to him before he had even stepped inside.

Novelist, playwright and essayist, Galsworthy was wealthy and at the height of his success. His early reputation was as a playwright but it is as a novelist that he is now chiefly remembered. The Forsyte family made its first appearance in a short story in 1901. The first novel of the Forsyte Saga, *A Man of Property*, appeared in 1906 and the family was to appear in further novels the later of which were written at Bury. The family has also appeared in two television adaptations, one in recent years, and at least one film version.

Galsworthy was awarded the Nobel prize for literature in 1932. His ashes were scattered on the Downs above Bury.

The words of E V Lucas again: Galsworthy was *"Always calm, always just, always courteous, and always surrounded by beautiful things..."*

Hilaire Belloc described the Roman Villa at Bignor as *"the place where some dead Roman had his palace built, near the soldier's road, in a place that looks at a great hollow of the Downs and is haunted by the ruin of fifteen hundred years."* In a novel, *The Three Gentlemen* (1932) by A E W Mason (1865-1948), a young Roman officer, Attilus Scaurus, is posted to the Sixth Legion in Britain which works as part of its duties, on the new road between Chichester and London: 'the soldiers' road: the road that the Saxons named and that we still call Stane Street. Unfortunately he is murdered but the story does not end there as he is reincarnated in episodes in the Elizabethan era and the modern time when Mason wrote the novel.

Author of crime novels featuring Inspector Hanaud of the Sureté and books of adventure, including *The Four Feathers* (1902) that has been filmed on a number of occasions, most recently in 2002, Mason's life would not be out of place in one of his novels. Unsuccessful as an actor, in addition to writing he became traveller, mountaineer, ocean yachtsman and Member of Parliament. He served in the Secret Service in the First World War as an eccentric Englishman cruising in a steam yacht off Spain and Morocco keeping an eye on enemy shipping. When he was uncovered by the Germans in that role, posing as a lepidopterist he went to Mexico where he discovered a clandestine enemy radio station and put it out of action.

It is a temptation sometimes when writing about literary figures to come across and eulogise one that the world has almost forgotten and who should, perhaps, remain that way. There are some, however, who are now little remembered but who not only had an influence in their day but also a story to tell. Charlotte Smith (1749-1806) was one of these. She was born at a time when the artistic accomplishments of a young lady should not be flaunted in public, still less for money, and when a married woman's rights were sparse.

Following marriage, unless protected by formal legal settlements, the province of the wealthy, a woman's property and income belonged automatically to her husband and the custody of any children was legally the husband's even on separation.

When Charlotte was three her mother died. Her father went travelling leaving Charlotte and younger sister and brother to spend their earlier formative years in the care of their aunt at Bignor Park. There, in a happy childhood in the freedom of the Sussex countryside she gained the foundation for her love of nature and the Sussex landscape that was to be reflected in her writing, and she was brought up in a world of fashion, elegance and wit. She was married two months short of her sixteenth birthday. She was beautiful and fashionable but not well supplied with money. She was later to say that she had been *"sold, a legal prostitute."* Her husband had prospects but was a spendthrift whose main accomplishment appears to have been the fathering of the children. She was to have a total of twelve children with eight babies during the first nine years of marriage. She was to spend time with her husband in the King's Bench Prison when he was committed there for debt. She was forced to follow her husband to France when he fled there to avoid his creditors and the bailiffs. Support was also lost when her wealthy father-in-law died leaving a will that was intended to help but was so convoluted that its settlement was to form a backdrop for the rest of her life giving her an absolute distaste for the legal profession. It is not surprising that more than a hint of melancholy runs through her poetry.

She was forced to find means to support her family. At first this came from the successful publication of her poetry and later, after the separation from her husband of twenty two years, from novels and children's books. As with other writers of the day especially the incoming Romantic movement, of which she was a forerunner, she was radical in her political opinion which is also reflected in her work. Like Wordsworth she was in favour of the French Revolution until it turned to terror.

As a novelist she was admired by Walter Scott and Jane Austen who was influenced by her: as a poet by William Wordsworth who described her as *"a lady to whom English verse is under greater obligations than are likely to be either acknowledged or remembered."* And so it was: her memory has faded. Although she was writing at a time when there was a well established tradition of women authors, literature was nevertheless male dominated.

DUNCTON TO CHARLTON

With your back to The Cricketers turn right and follow the concrete path between the hedgerow and the main road, heading north. In 50m reach Dyehouse Lane and turn right following the bridleway signs.

Walk past 'Wild Cherries' as the broad track drops and swings right. Cross a small stream and climb up towards Duncton Mill Trout Fishery.

The watermill you see to your left was built in 1824, but has not been used for nearly a hundred years, although there are hopes that it may be refurbished one day. The beautiful farmhouse is somewhat earlier and dates from 1767; it operated as a farm until the lakes were built about twenty-five years ago. Now, during the summer, this is a 'members only' trout fishery – and is very popular. The lakes are gradually being extended and the fish seem to be getting bigger, with a 9lb 14oz catch being recorded recently.

In 2004 Mike Boxhall, an international teacher of many years' standing, found his dream location here for his advanced courses in Craniosacral Therapy and the residential centre is now available for many sorts of courses and conferences. Several of the other attractive buildings are also available as 'holiday lets' – a perfect retreat in this most peaceful corner of Sussex.

The Trail passes besides the crystal clear waters of the upper lake and then climbs a little more steeply to reach a public road. Here turn right.

The fine views from here are of Seaford College ahead and the relay aerial on Bexleyhill, just north of Midhurst, away to the right.

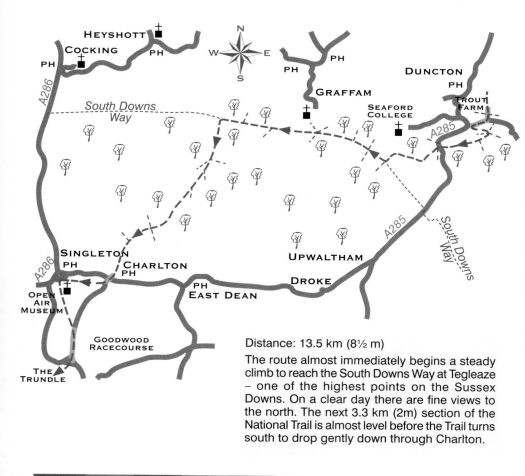

Distance: 13.5 km (8½ m)

The route almost immediately begins a steady climb to reach the South Downs Way at Tegleaze – one of the highest points on the Sussex Downs. On a clear day there are fine views to the north. The next 3.3 km (2m) section of the National Trail is almost level before the Trail turns south to drop gently down through Charlton.

5 KM

3 MILES

In 300m, besides the 'give way' sign of the main A285, turn left following the bridleway sign through a wooden gate and begin climbing up through the trees. The Trail swings left and unexpectedly reaches an old limekiln.

Lime has always been important in both building and farming and the Romans knew about chalk burning. In the middle ages it was produced in kilns like these by burning the chalk from the South Downs.

The resulting calcium oxide is a nasty, unstable substance more commonly known as quick lime. It is stabilised by adding water to make it 'slaked lime'. Mixed with sand and ash this makes a strong mortar, and can also be used to correct acidity as a fertiliser in the land. If a stick of quick lime is heated in an oxy-hydrogen flame it gives off an intense white light. This was much used in theatres and is better known as 'limelight'.

The Trail now zigzags to the right and leads uphill for a further 10 minutes or so and then begins to level out. Finally on a level section it reaches a post on which there are blue arrows. Turn sharp right to face a choice of two paths. Take the left hand one of these which heads more steeply uphill. (The compass bearing is due west – 270°). Shortly ignore a bridleway to the left and continue uphill. In 350m the path will level out and emerge from the trees to continue straight ahead across an open field. On reaching the main road turn right and in just 50m cross the road carefully and walk up the tarmac drive towards 'Duncton Minerals'. On reaching the metal gate at the quarry entrance, swing left following the broad

track heading uphill indicated by a red arrow.

At one point there is a good view of the deep quarry down to the right illustrating clearly that these hills are almost entirely chalk. This is one of the few quarries still being worked.

The track levels off and opens out and soon, where there is a fork, keep left and continue heading slightly uphill to reach the crossing South Downs Way at Tegleaze Post.

'TEG' is a Sussex dialect word, first used in the 16th century, for a young sheep. The second part of the name simply means pasture. In 1793 the Rev. Arthur Young estimated that there were upwards of 340,000 sheep in Sussex and he vividly described the flocks at the time as: "A moving dung-hill, manuring the land without any expense." Quite.

Turn right along the National Trail as it heads westwards going slightly downhill. Follow the Trail for 1.7 kms (about 25 / 30 minutes steady walking) with several open fields to your right. Where these open fields come to an end there are two five-armed fingerposts, the one on the left being to the memory of a founder member of the 'Sussex Downsmen' back in 1923. Now renamed the South Downs Society, its prime concern remains the protection of the unique landscape of the South Downs.

Continue ahead along the South Downs Way into what is now known as the 'wooded section'.

Follow the National Trail along this level section for a further 1.6 kms and at the end of the new 'green

corridor', a cleared area to the right of the Trail, look for a three armed fingerpost on the left with a bridleway going left downhill into Charlton Forest. For clarity, the path you must take to the left passes between two raised earth banks – here to prevent motorised access.

You are now entering the depths of Charlton Forest, an area made famous by hunting and smuggling – two activities with an unexpected connection. King Charles II had several illegitimate sons, two of who became closely associated with this area. One was the Duke of Monmouth who was a joint founder of the 'Charlton Hunt' in the mid 1600's. This was to become the most fashionable hunt in all of England. Another of the sons was the first Duke of Richmond who bought a nearby hunting lodge called 'Goodwood' in 1697. His son, the Second Duke, was also a great lover of hunting and it was he who was largely responsible for bringing the notorious Hawkhurst Gang to justice.

This infamous Kent-based gang of smugglers exercised a reign of terror along the whole of the south east coast of England. It has been said that they could raise the help of no less than 500 men within an hour's notice. However, following a gang meeting in Charlton Forest on 4th October 1747, things got out of hand with the particularly gruesome murder of a customs officer and an informer. For this crime four of the gang were gibbeted – one of them on The Trundle, which the Trail passes a few miles further on. It was the beginning of the end for the gang.

The track soon broadens as it descends and crosses a wide forest ride. In a further 750m after passing a broad drive off to the left the track forks – take the left fork – and in just another 100m take the narrower bridleway, marked by a fingerpost, to the right. After 450m the path levels off and you must now look carefully for a footpath fingerpost to the right. Take this level path heading slightly off to the right. It eventually converges with a broad forest ride. Continue ahead along the broad ride and in another 250m keep left on a waymarked footpath heading very

slightly uphill. Cross straight over the next crossing footpath and head downhill to reach a stile into an open field. Cross diagonally over this field with views of Levin Down ahead and on reaching the hedgeline on the far side follow it to the right. At the end of the hedge follow it around to the left to cross a stile and wind steeply down a grassy meadow and cross another stile to meet a hard surfaced bridleway.

Turn left along this track and in a further 1km reach North Lane at Charlton. The 'Fox Goes Free' is just 100m along the road to your left.

Formally known as the 'Pig & Whistle' the inn changed its name to The Fox when the Duke of Richmond popularised hunting in the area – the last bit was added when the pub became a 'free house'. It was here in November 1915 that the Singleton & East Dean Women's Institute held the first ever formal meeting in England of a W.I. The institute was formed to help the war effort, mainly with agricultural work and helping convalescent soldiers.

OVER THE DOWNS

William Cobbett rode westwards from Billingshurst to Petworth. After spending the night there he turned southwards towards the South Downs. Shortly after setting out he met two men hoeing turnips who assured him that it would not rain. But, soon afterwards, he saw *"beginning to poke up over the South Downs (then right before me) several parcels of those white, curled clouds, that we call* Judges' Wigs. *And they are just like judges' wigs. Not the* parson-like *things which the judges wear when they have to listen to the dull wrangling and duller jests of the lawyers; but those* big *wigs which hang down about their shoulders when they are about to tell you a little of* their intentions*, and when their very looks say,* "Stand clear!*" These clouds (if rising from the south-west) hold precisely the same language to the great-coatless traveller. Rain is* sure *to follow them."*

And so it was. Cobbett ascended Duncton Hill by the high road *"which is obliged to go twisting about"* to get to the top of the ridge but, before he got to the top, *"the white clouds had become black, had spread themselves all around, and a pretty decent and sturdy rain began to fall"*; weather that is not unknown on the Downs. A small side road, before the main road is reached and begins *"twisting about"* up Duncton Hill, leads up towards Woolavington Church.

How far does a prince of the church fit onto a Literary Trail? There certainly would have been sermons and pastoral letters and there were other religious and polemical works sufficient to merit an entry in the *Oxford Companion of English Literature*.

Edward Henry Manning was born in 1808, educated at Harrow and Balliol College, Oxford. Gladstone, a contemporary at Oxford, thought that Manning was one of the three handsomest men at Oxford. It was originally intended that he would enter politics but the loss of the family money led to his ordination into the Church of England in 1833, his first appointment being as curate to John Sargent, rector of Woolavington and Graffham.

Manning married Caroline, the rector's daughter, and when the rector died, Manning succeeded him as rector. One of the churches under his care was Woolavington, the small church that lies under the lip of the Downs close behind Lavington House. Lavington House was once the home of the Buchanans, the distillers of Black & White whiskey, but now forms part of Seaford College to which the church is the chapel.

PUNCH'S FANCY PORTRAITS.—No. 113.

HIS EMINENCE CARDINAL MANNING.
(Regarding a Fancy Portrait of what he might have been.)
AND IN SPITE OF ALL TEMPTATIONS,
IF YOU READ HIS "PROTESTATIONS,"
HE REMAINS "AN ENGLISHMAN."
(Vide an "Englishman's Protest" in the "Nineteenth Century.")

Manning was set to rise high within the Church of England but Caroline died four years after the marriage. She was buried at the little church. Manning was appointed archdeacon of Chichester in 1840 but rose no further in the Church of England. Doubts about his vocation had also set in. He crossed to Rome in 1851 and was ordained as a Catholic priest. Within 14 years he had become the Archbishop of Westminster and was made a Cardinal in 1875.

He served both his church and his country being a member of the royal commissions on the housing of the poor in 1885 and education in 1886. His enlightened political thinking and actions influenced many including Hilaire Belloc. When Manning died in 1892, the four mile route from church to cemetery was continuously lined by mourners, not all of them Catholic.

It has been said that he forgot his wife and that her grave was neglected as he rose within a church with a celibate clergy but the book in which she had written her meditations was at his bedside for the remainder of his life after she died.

And of the Downs he wrote, "*...the Downs seem to be only less beautiful than Heaven.*"

Hilaire Belloc has been with us for much of the way. Although *The Four Men* do represent facets of his personality we have yet to hear much of the man himself. He could, however, make an appropriate appearance at any stage along the Trail from beginning to end. He was a man of the whole of Sussex. He lived in the village of Shipley but cannot be mainly associated with any part of Sussex.

At the start of the Trail in Horsham the Black Horse Hotel once stood at the south west corner of Lynd Cross where Shelley's Fountain is now the centrepiece. The Black Horse (see page 6) was replaced in 1964 by the shops and offices that now stand there. It is commemorated in the name of a nearby street and was one of Belloc's regular haunts in later life when age and infirmity impeded the wide travels that had been part of his life. Of Chichester, at the other end of the Trail, he wrote that it was, "...*a town which I should know best in Europe, for it was the market town and local capital of my youth, ...*" He had spent that youth at Slindon, a village about six miles outside Chichester. But for now he is on Duncton Hill. In his poem of that title, one of those expressive of his feelings for Sussex, he is that "*boy that sings on Duncton Hill.*"

> "*So, therefore, though myself be cross*
> *The shuddering of that dreadful day*
> *When friend and fire and home are lost*
> *And even children drawn away –*
> *The passer-by shall hear me still,*
> *A boy that sings on Duncton Hill.*"

Belloc's work, like the man, was wide ranging. His verse includes the nonsense and the paeans to Sussex already mentioned. There are also the Cautionary Tales with the awful fates that befell such as Jim who ran away from his nurse and was eaten by a lion and Matilda who told such *Dreadful Lies*, and was *Burned to Death*. There are also the celebrations of life and people and places. There is even a letter in verse to E V Lucas asking why he did not come to see Belloc and giving precise directions how to get there including the amount of the bus fare. There are the intricate and compelling rhythms of *Tarantella*, perhaps his most famous poem, evoking the dim, smoky interior of the Spanish inn with a dancer swirling and the sound of the music above the hum of talk.

> "*Do you remember an Inn, Miranda?*
> *Do you remember an Inn?*
> *And the tedding and the spreading*
> *Of the straw for a bedding,*
> *And the fleas that tease in the High Pyrenees*
> *And the wine that tasted of the tar?*"

But who was Miranda? Belloc had two great loves in his life but neither of those was Miranda. They were Sussex and his wife Elodie.

A N Wilson, Belloc's biographer, argues that Miranda was almost certainly a man. Belloc would never have taken a young woman to such an inn. The poem 'eulogises' "*male friendship and the excitement of foreign travel.*" Belloc said that he chose the name for its rhythm and sound but he did know a Spanish diplomat, the Duke of Miranda, and that may have brought the name to Belloc's mind.

"When he addressed Miranda, he could have been addressing a dozen dead companions who would go walking and drinking with him no more."

Belloc's output was huge. Once, it is said, whole library shelves were devoted to his work. Well over a hundred books included the poetry, travel, biography, essays, novels, religion, politics, the First World War and, of course, Sussex. His best remembered and possibly best book is *The Path to Rome* (1902). It was probably his favourite too. He said that it was the only book that he wrote for love rather than for the money that he needed to support himself and his family. It must also stand as the symbol for his prodigious walking. It tells of his walk to Rome from Toul, the town where he had been stationed during his service with the French army. He had been an artilleryman one of the three riding a team of horses pulling a field gun. He was not well equipped in modern terms for the trip. He wore a thin linen suit *"that originally cost not ten shillings"* and carried *"in a small bag or pocket slung over (his) shoulder, a large piece of bread, half a pound of smoked ham, a sketch-book, two Nationalist papers, and a quart of the wine of Brulé."* He took the straightest line that he could, going over rather than round mountains and suffering harsh weather with nothing to cover his body other than that thin suit. He made Rome but this story could have ended in a tragic fashion on the way.

Joseph Hilaire Pierre Belloc was born on 27th July 1870 at the village of La Celle Saint Cloud twelve miles outside Paris during a thunderstorm. This led to his mother calling him "Old Thunder" particularly when his temper erupted. His mother was English from a literary and political background that was to permeate Belloc's upbringing. His father was French: a lawyer of poor health but also with literary connections. He died young in 1872 at the age of forty-two.

Having escaped out of France on the outbreak of the Franco-Prussian War three days after Hilaire Belloc's birth, the family were able to live in some style in London, but economies became necessary when much of the widowed Mrs Belloc's fortune disappeared with her stockbroker. To avoid the expense of maintaining a substantial house in London the family moved to Slindon five days before Belloc's eighth birthday. It was there walking on the Downs above and beyond Slindon, from Petersfield to Beachy Head, that his great love affair with Sussex began.

After being educated at the Oratory School in Birmingham under Cardinal Newman, openings in a number of careers beckoned. He experienced the French Navy, land agency, draughtsmanship and journalism. None of these lasted for long, although he was to illustrate some of his books and writing for magazines and newspapers was to be part of his life.

In 1890, Mrs Ellen Hogan of Napa, California brought her two daughters, Elizabeth and Elodie to Europe. During their stay in London they met the Belloc family. It may not have been love at first sight between Elodie and Belloc but love certainly grew in the six weeks that they were together before she had to return to America although her feelings then, and later, were complicated by her belief that she had a vocation to become a nun. They wrote to each other and the following year Belloc, whose financial position was somewhat precarious, as it was to be for most of his life, borrowed £20 and sold books precious to him (although Mrs Belloc was to find out and buy them back), to enable him to sail the Atlantic and cross the United States to forward his suit. Tradition has it that he walked across America to reach Elodie. More prosaically he reached California by train although he walked in much of America as he returned homewards after he had been rejected. Elodie's mother was much opposed and she was still troubled by the possibility of a vocation. They did continue to write frequently to each other and were finally to marry five years later.

In the intervening years he volunteered for and completed his service for a year with the French Army. Although military service was compulsory for French citizens there was no need for Belloc to have undertaken it. Volunteering may have been on the rebound from Elodie's refusal. His mother thought that it was a mistake and that it would mark him as a foreigner in any subsequent career in England. Belloc believed in later years that she had been right. Three years study at Balliol College in the University of Oxford culminating in a First Class Degree in history followed military service. He made his mark at the University.

He was more mature with a wider experience than his fellow undergraduates. He has already adopted the characteristic mode of dressing that was to remain with him for life: a dark cloak and a wide brimmed hat.

He broke the record for walking to London. He was said to be the best speaker in the Oxford Union since Gladstone and joined very distinguished company, past and future, when he was elected President of the Union.

It was a bitter disappointment that was to effect him until the end of his days that he was not elected to be a Fellow of All Souls College after his brilliant undergraduate career and First Class Degree. That, at the least, would have led to an academic career that could have provided a measure of security. Nevertheless he set out again by sea and railway on the long journey to Elodie whose attempted entry into a convent had been little short of disastrous. She accepted him. They were married at Napa on 15th June 1896 and they returned to England where the proceeds of *The Bad Child's Book of Beasts* (1896) helped to alleviate their financial situation.

It was in 1906 that they came to the village of Shipley on their search for a Sussex home: Belloc in the saddle of a large bicycle with Elodie being pulled in a wickerwork trailer behind. Kings Land with its adjoining windmill captured them as soon as they saw it. It had no 'mod cons', and it was not to everybody's taste even years later when those conveniences had been provided, but it was the only home that either of them was to know from then on.

Marriage did not slow Belloc down. He still travelled widely and wrote much. In 1906 he increased the burden by standing in Salford as a parliamentary candidate for the Liberal Party and was elected. He was returned as Member for Salford in the election that was called in 1910 as a result of the House of Lords rejecting Lloyd George's budget: an action that was to intensify the long and continued pressure for the reform of the House of Lords that still rumbles on. He was not willing, however, to stand again in the election that was called later in 1910 unless as an independent. That was not to be.

There may have been an element of boredom in not wanting to prolong his parliamentary life but he was disillusioned by a party system where the leaders of both main parties were the friends and relations of each other, mixing in the same social circles, attending the same events and house parties and shoots. There was corruption too and secretive political funding even then.

His five acres in Sussex gave sanctuary from the cut and thrust of politics when he was in Parliament. They always provided stability in a crowded life. Not all was laughter and song. Elodie died on 2nd December 1914 aged 42. Her body was removed from her bedroom and Belloc locked its door. It was not entered again during Belloc's lifetime. For nearly forty years every time that he passed that door he kissed or traced the sign of the cross on it. His eldest son Louis was killed in the First World War, his younger son, Peter, in the Second.

Throughout his life he had a conversational presence that has been likened to that of Dr Johnson and a infinite capacity for friendship: friends old and new, male and female, of all degrees, with those of a completely opposite view. There were the sad times but there was also merriment, company and wine.

Belloc kept up a punishing schedule but the years did begin to take their toll. On reaching the age of 60 he wrote, "*I get older every year, oddly enough, instead of staying the same as one does between 20 and 60.*" And his comments on his 67th birthday in 1937 will strike a distinct chord for those of us who walk and who are finding that the same hills are getting higher and steeper than we remembered them. A sailor as well as a walker, he had made a channel crossing with his son and some other 'young men': "*I am too old to go to sea in small boats that jump up and down. And every year I say I won't go again. And every year I go for a 'once more' and I get stiffer and stiffer every time.*"

He died on 15th July 1953 after a fall at Kings Land a few days before his 83rd birthday. More than one of his obituaries described him as the "*last of the giants*".

There are views northwards from the ridge at the top of the escarpment. These include Blackdown, the highest point in Sussex, where Alfred, Lord Tennyson (1809-92), made his final home at Aldworth, the house that was built to his design, on a clearing that had once been used as a potato field.

Tennyson was a celebrity in the days when celebrities had something to celebrate. He was one of the few poets who reached fame and fortune.

Although he was already an established poet when Queen Victoria ascended the throne in 1837, he almost spanned the Victorian age, dying nine years before the Queen herself having, unlike Belloc, reached the age of 83. And, as he overshadowed the Weald of Sussex and the Downs beyond from Blackdown, so he overshadowed the poetry of his contemporaries. There was no-one who could match him and although he may be viewed as a symbol of Victoriana, his verse is not heavy with a brooding morality covering a life of nineteenth century hypocrisy.

He was appointed Poet Laureate in 1850 in succession to William Wordsworth whose court dress, now on display at the Wordsworth Museum in Grasmere in the Lake District, he borrowed for his own investiture. But he was painfully shy and, as his fame grew, he sought to preserve his privacy, usually in vain. In 1852 he came to the Isle of Wight looking for a house where he could find solitude. He first leased and then bought the house, Farringford, but his fame still grew and the crowds still came to view him. In 1854 there came *The Charge of the Light Brigade*. Tennyson then really became a national poet perhaps not only from the nationalistic sentiment but from the understanding that all was not well: "*Someone had blundered*": at first the establishment persuaded Tennyson to remove those words but he later put them back.

People peered in at him through his windows pressing their faces against the glass. When he went for a walk, crowds followed him across the Isle of Wight Downs. Tennyson once complained to Queen Victoria, another habitual visitor to the Isle of Wight, of the barbarous invasions to his privacy. When she said that she had no such trouble in the Isle of Wight, he replied to the effect that no doubt if he could post a sentry with a gun at his gate, he would have no trouble either.

So he came to Aldworth on Blackdown, although he still returned to the Isle of Wight out of season to the end of his life.

"Our birches yellowing and from each
The light leaf falling fast,
While squirrels from our fiery beech
Were bearing off the mast,
You came, and look'd and loved the view
Long-known and loved by me,
Green Sussex fading into blue
With one gray glimpse of sea."

It was from Aldworth that "*one gray glimpse of sea*" was caught in the lines best known in Sussex.

He died at Aldworth. He was buried in Westminster Abbey. The aisle was lined with survivors who had charged with the Light Brigade forty years before.

But was there something to hide in the search for seclusion?

The Rt. Revd. Monsignor Ronald Knox (1868-1957) was a son an Anglican Bishop of Manchester but converted to Roman Catholicism where he entered the priesthood and was later awarded the honorary papal title of 'Monsignor' that is conferred on those who are highly regarded. He was a friend of Hilaire Belloc, a frequent visitor to Kings Land and an author in his own right. He was once described as "*the wickedest clerk in Holy Orders*", not for his life of sin but for his satirical wit. It was in his book *Essays in Satire* (1928) that he explored the true authorship of what has been attributed to Tennyson as perhaps his greatest poem, *In Memoriam,* that commemorates the early death of Tennyson's great friend, Arthur Hallam, and is said to have taken seventeen years in the writing.

It is now widely fashionable to seek and find codes, Da Vincian and otherwise, in all manner of texts and, with modern computers, it is becoming increasingly easy to find what one is seeking whether it was intentional or not. But such messages have always been sought. In an essay Knox outlines the painstaking analysis that he undertook well in advance of the current fascination uncovering Tennyson as, in this case, an illusion, masking the pen of the then occupant of the throne, Queen Victoria herself.

The Trail descends from the Downs into the valley of the River Lavant where it turns right, westwards, to Singleton before ascending to St Roche's Hill crowned by the Iron Age fort of The Trundle. If one turns instead to the left along the road that runs through the valley past The Fox Goes Free, one reaches East Dean, another of those flint-walled Sussex villages nestling in a fold in the Downs. Here the playwright, Christopher Fry (1907-2005), had his home.

Fry's first career was as a school master but he gave that up to found a theatre company in Tunbridge Wells which he ran for three years. He went on to write lyrics and music for the stage including that of London's West End. It was a Sussex vicar who changed Fry's focus when he asked Fry to write a play about a Sussex saint, St Cuthman. The play is *The Boy with a Cart* (1939). It tells how Cuthman was called in 7th century Saxon England to preach the word of God. He took to the roads to seek alms. His mother travelled with him in that cart, a handcart that Cuthman pushed, or pulled, (versions differ) aided by a rope slung around his shoulders to support the weight. When the replacement rope that Cuthman had had to improvise finally and irretrievably broke at Steyning, he took that as a sign from God and founded his church there. His statue faces the 12th century stone church that replaces Cuthman's simple building.

Fry wished to serve when the Second World War broke out but did not want to shoot people. T S Eliot, with whom he was to cause a revival in English verse drama, suggested the fire service, and when told that Fry had no head for heights advised that he "*must specialise in basements.*"

After the War and service in the Pioneer Corps Fry returned to writing. His sparkling words and wit and the glittering productions of his plays were part of that revival and an antidote to the austerity of the war years. It was a joke by the speech writers for Margaret Thatcher (as she then was) based on the title of Fry's most widely remembered play, *The Lady's not for Burning* (1949), that later gave rise to her best known quotation, "*You turn if you want to, the lady's not for turning.*"

He became, however, submerged in the gritty realism of 'kitchen sink' drama of the 1950s although he still continued to work: plays, translations, film scripts. The film *Ben-Hur* was nominated in 1959 for twelve Academy Awards. It won a then unprecedented eleven Oscars apart from best screenplay. Only one writer was credited. It was not Fry even though having been invited to write the final part of the script he ended by virtually rewriting the whole. The members of the Academy may have been well aware of the welter of controversy that surrounded the issue. It may also be ironic that in the same year Simone Signoret was awarded the Oscar for best actress for her performance in the film version of *Room at the Top*, part of the wave of social realism.

And the work continued into the twenty-first century. His play *A Ringing of Bells* (2001) was staged at London's Olivier theatre.

Charlton to Chichester

From North Lane cross straight over the main road, following the sign 'Goodwood 1m'. Almost unnoticed, the road crosses the fledgling River Lavant which, being a 'winterbourne' is rarely seen flowing in summer. In a further 50m as the road bears left look for a fingerpost on the right. Follow this across the open field with a fence line to your left and fine views of Levin Down now to your right. At the end of this long field pass through a kissing gate and turn quickly right then left to follow a path between houses.

Cross straight over the next public road into The Leys and at the end of the short cul-de-sac look for an archway to the right of the house marked 'Church Way 1-11'. Go through the archway and pass directly in front of the two terraced houses to reach an open path leading to the church.

Singleton Church is the oldest building in this valley with a fine 10th century Saxon tower. The remaining foundations of the original nave are also over a thousand years old. The name of the village derives from the old words 'sengel' and 'ton' and literally means 'the settlement in a burnt clearing' – indicating that this whole area was once densely forested.

Keep straight ahead past the entrance to the church (a right turn here would lead to The Partridge Inn) and walk between a stone wall on the right and a hedge on your left.

Turn left following the stone wall, but keeping inside the churchyard and exit through a gate to pass the large farm buildings to your right. Cross a stile besides a metal gate and begin climbing. The path becomes quite steep for 250m before gradually easing off as Goodwood Racecourse comes into view.

To your right now, behind the trees, is the Singleton Open Air Museum – opened to the public in 1971. Here, set in 50 acres of countryside, there is a fascinating collection of nearly 50 historic buildings dating from the 13th to the 19th century together with farm animals, woodland walks and a picturesque lake.

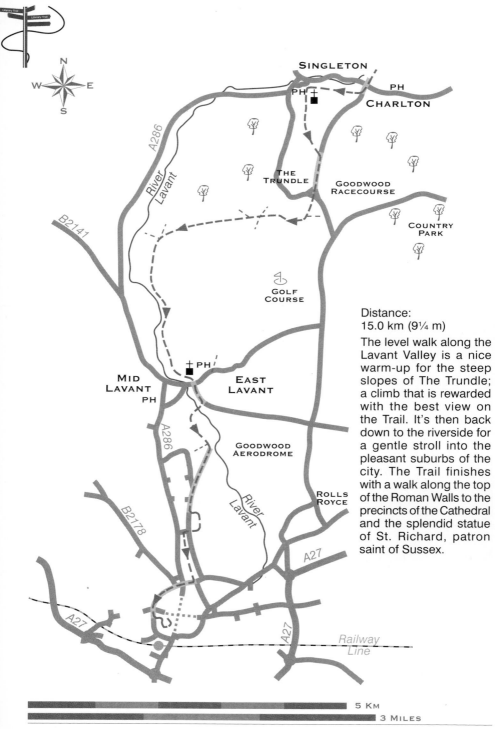

Distance:
15.0 km (9¼ m)

The level walk along the Lavant Valley is a nice warm-up for the steep slopes of The Trundle; a climb that is rewarded with the best view on the Trail. It's then back down to the riverside for a gentle stroll into the pleasant suburbs of the city. The Trail finishes with a walk along the top of the Roman Walls to the precincts of the Cathedral and the splendid statue of St. Richard, patron saint of Sussex.

5 KM

3 MILES

The buildings have all been carefully dismantled and rebuilt to their original form and bring to life the homes, farmsteads and rural industries of the last 500 years. A visit needs plenty of time.

Follow the clear path to a stile leading onto the public road and turn right towards The Trundle. Enter the car park at the road junction ahead and keep to the left side of it. Exit through the car park entrance and cross the main road carefully to a flight of steps opposite heading steeply uphill. Turn left at the kissing gate and follow a grassy track to the top of The Trundle.

This is the site of a Neolithic causewayed camp from around 4,000BC. It was enlarged and converted later to an Iron Age hill fort and later still acquired the name St Roche's Hill where there was a 14th century chapel. In more recent times there was a windmill, which sadly burnt down in 1773.

Our Trail briefly joins the Monarch's Way here – the route to exile taken by the twenty one year old King Charles 11 after his defeat at the Battle of Worcester in 1651. Until recently his escape was celebrated every year on 29th May – the King's birthday. It was called 'Oak Apple Day' in memory of him famously hiding in the Boscobel Oak Tree. It later became known as 'Pinch Bum Day'; something to do with what happened if you didn't bring an oak apple to school that day!

Walk up onto the highest rampart and follow this around to the south and west with magnificent views of Chichester, the south coast and the Isle of Wight.

The Duke of Richmond brought horse racing to his estate in 1802. Today Goodwood is probably the most beautiful setting for any permanent racecourse in the world, and the glorious meeting is very popular with the creme of society who consume 20,000 bottles of champagne during the 20 race days. Lester Piggott, arguably the best-known British jockey of all time, rode 197 winners at Goodwood during his career.

On reaching the western gap in the rampart drop down onto a broad flint path where there is a wooden bench. Pass through a kissing gate besides the wooden gate and walk downhill heading west. Go through a second kissing gate to Seven Paths car park and at the tarmac road ahead go straight over following the bridleway sign towards West Dean. Walk past the Old Rubbing House (where horses were rubbed down after their long climb) and at the bridleway junction ahead keep left staying level.

Gently descend downhill for 1 km to pass through a gate where there is a fine view of the Lavant Valley and turn half left heading down a grassy track across a wide, open field. At the bottom of the hill reach a four-armed post and turn left before the fence. In 20m pass through a gate and head south down the valley floor with a fence to your right. After passing through a further gate the path narrows between trees and soon touches the banks of the River Lavant.

Some years ago, this tiny 'winterbourne' caused an amazing amount of damage to the valley and surrounding area.

The autumn of 1993 was exceptionally wet and flooding was first recorded in late December in the area just north of the A27 bypass, to the east of Chichester. By the end of the year the river was running bank-full and, within a week, the A27 bypass itself was flooded and was closed. Sewage then began to back up at Singleton. The next day the A259 was also closed.

Rain continued to fall for a further 11 days and the flooding became more widespread. A 'Bailey Bridge' was erected by the army to open the A259, but the flooding on the A27 was too great to be bridged and, for some days, the only safe route across West Sussex was via the M25 motorway just south of London. By the end of January the water had subsided. Forty-five houses had been flooded in the upper catchment villages, as well as large areas of farmland and many local roads. Trains had operated at reduced speed, since the stability of the railway embankments had been threatened. The little winterbourne had shown its teeth.

Pass by a concrete bridge and continue ahead with the river to your right. As you approach the houses at East Lavant the broad track swings to the left away from the river and emerges into the village by Staple House Farm. Cross the river bridge to the road and turn left along Sheep Wash Lane. Join the main road by the war memorial and keep left along Pook Lane to cross the road bridge over the river. Opposite St Mary's Church turn right down Fordwater Road. At this point the Royal Oak pub & restaurant is 150m ahead along Pook Lane.

Walk south along the public road and 150m after passing the last farm building turn right following a footpath fingerpost through a gate and cross the open field to the river. Cross the river on a metal bridge and turn half left across the next field. The path swings left and passes through a gate now heading south towards the houses. Just before the houses it turns right then immediately left to follow a hedgeline. Go to the left of the tall wooden fence ahead to reach a public road.

Turn right along the road for 600m to reach the busy main Summersdale Road and continue straight ahead. In a further 250m walk past the entrance to Fordwater School. At the next road after the school turn left. Where the road opens out with a playing field to the right, turn right and follow the paved path with the playing field now to your left.

The buildings away to your left were those of Graylingwell Hospital which first opened its doors in Chichester in 1897 to house the pauper lunatics of West Sussex. Various additions and extensions were made, most notably the wards build in the 30's to deal with a need to increase capacity on the site. During the First World War the buildings were converted for use as a military hospital to treat the many wounded men returning form France. At the end of the war the site was returned to public use as an asylum and remained so until 2002. The hospital was officially closed a year later and the site has been renamed '9 College Lane'.

This meets a tarmac drive opposite Connolly House and here turn right back onto the main road. Cross carefully straight over into Wellington Road and in 75m, just past the entrance to the rugby club, turn left through a gap into the park. Walk down the left hand side of the rugby pitches of Oakland's Park, with a splendid view of the Cathedral ahead, and pass to the left of the Festival Theatre.

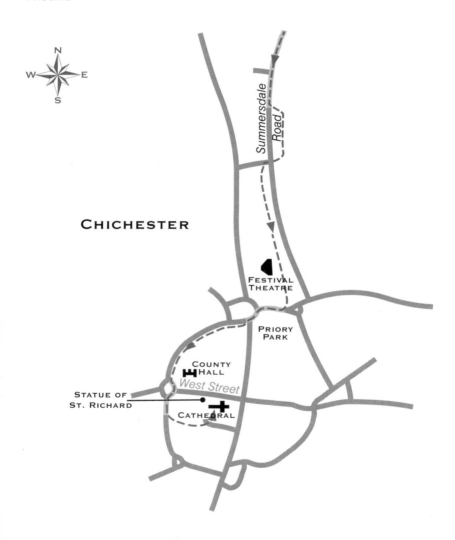

CHICHESTER

Summersdale Road

FESTIVAL THEATRE

PRIORY PARK

COUNTY HALL

West Street

STATUE OF ST. RICHARD

CATHEDRAL

500 M

½ MILE

Chichester Festival Theatre was designed by British architects Powell & Moya, well known for many of their 'Oxbridge' college buildings, and opened in 1962 with much anticipation and to great acclaim for its founder Leslie Evershed-Martin CBE.

Laurence Olivier was the first artistic director and it soon became one of the UK's flagship theatres with an international reputation for creating magical live performances. It was here that the first National Theatre Company was formed and several productions were transferred from Chichester to the Old Vic in London.

With 1,206 seats, it was the first modern theatre in this country to have an open 'thrust' stage with the audience seated around it on three sides allowing them a much closer involvement with the actors than with a traditional proscenium arch stage; here the audience and artists are all in the same room. The festival 'season' runs from April to September and includes productions from classics to contemporary writing and musicals.

Walk between the tennis courts and the car park. At the far side of the car park exit onto the dual carriageway and turn right along the pavement to reach the underpass. Take this under the main road and on the far side turn right and then bear left to walk into Northgate, following the sign to 'Pedestrian Area'. In just 35m turn right into North Walls keeping to the right and climb up onto the old city walls. Follow the walls walk around behind County Hall to emerge at Westgate opposite the Chichester Inn.

(The route from here is through the Bishop's Palace Gardens, the gates to which are closed at dusk. If you are late arriving turn left in front of the Chichester Inn and walk down West Street to the Cathedral.) Otherwise, cross straight over into Avenue de Chartres and in 50m, just after the hotel car park, turn left besides a high flint wall following a sign to the Bishop's Palace Gardens.

The word 'palace' comes from the name of one of the seven hills of Rome – the Palatine Hill – where the original buildings were the seats of imperial power. In England, by tacit agreement, few buildings have been called 'palaces' other than those used as official residences for royalty and certain bishops. These royal and ecclesiastical palaces were not merely residences; the clerks who administered the realm or the diocese laboured there as well and, to this day, many bishops' palaces house both their family apartments and their official offices.

Turn right through a gate into the gardens and follow the path around to the left. Keep on the main path as it winds around the garden. Just past the entrance to the Bishop's Palace, turn left through a gap in the brick wall to the vegetable garden. Leave this small garden through a gate onto the drive to the Bishop's Palace and turn right under the tower.

In 50m, opposite the Deanery, turn left down St. Richard's Walk towards the Cathedral. On reaching the cloisters turn left to walk around the south wall of the Cathedral to the statue of Saint Richard.

This magnificent statue by Philip Jackson (Royal Sculptor to Queen Elizabeth II) was unveiled during the millennium celebrations. Jackson is noted for his modern style and emphasis on form and the work was a gift from the Friends of the Cathedral.

Richard de la Wych was probably born in Worcestershire, deriving his name from the mineral springs there, locally called 'wyches'. After his education at Oxford, Paris and Bologna, he was enthroned as Bishop of Chichester in 1245.

He died on 3rd April 1253 in the Maison Dieu at Dover and was canonised by the Pope as Saint Richard in 1261. Fifteen years later, his relics were removed from their first resting-place in the Cathedral to the shrine in the retrochoir where they remained until the Reformation. The shrine itself remains a place of pilgrimage.

St. Richard's statue marks the end of the West Sussex Literary Trail.

TO THE END

William Cobbett breakfasted at Singleton on the same day in 1823 that he had earlier ascended Duncton Hill. He was still wet from the soaking that he had received on the way. He did not go on to Chichester. He had no business there and it would have taken him too far to the south of his way.

He was impressed, however, with what he saw about him. *"The lane goes along through some of the finest farms in the world. It is impossible for corn land and for agriculture to be finer than these. ... There is besides, no misery to be seen here. I have seen no wretchedness in Sussex ... and as to these villages in the South Downs, they are beautiful to behold."*

Up on The Trundle there is another of those meetings of ways: with the Monarch's Way. A 610 mile (981 km) long distance footpath based on the route of the escape of the uncrowned King Charles II from defeat at the Battle of Worcester in 1651.

The novel *Ovingdean Grange: A Tale of the South Downs* (1860) by William Harrison Ainsworth (1805-1882), a dandy said to be one of the two best-looking and best dressed men in London, is centred on the escape of Charles II.

It was Ainsworth who created the legend of Dick Turpin's ride to York on Black Bess in *Rookwood* (1834). Such a feat did apparently happen but it was not Dick Turpin. Daniel Defoe (1660-1711) in his *Tour Through the Whole Island of Great Britain* (1724-6) attributed it to a highwayman called Nicks but others were also credited with it. The name of the horse is not recorded but, in Defoe's version, it is a bay.

Below The Trundle in 1915, D H Lawrence and Eleanor Farjeon, having found their way, continued on to Chichester. They "*saw the loop of the race-course in the hills*" but it was getting late and in Goodwood Park they "*began to drag (their) limbs. 'Please do not walk on the edges of the grass' said small notices.*" (Eleanor Farjeon) was "*grateful to the peer who did not warn the footsore off his grass altogether.*" She arrived in Chichester with a bad blister on her heel. Next day 'tramping' was out of the question. She could not put her foot to the ground in her heavy walking boot and left Chichester by train wearing a pair of 'sneakers' two sizes too big that she had been forced to buy.

In the 1930s walkers led by or following the directions of S P B (Stuart Petre Brodie) Mais (1885-1975) might have been encountered on or about The Trundle. It is he who must here stand as the representative of all who have led or devised walks and written about them.

He was another who came to Sussex and embraced it or was embraced by it: perhaps a mixture of both. He too was also one whose early career was in teaching but a career move to the Royal Air Force College at Cranwell was not a success when his more enlightened teaching methods did not find favour with the RAF of the early 1920s. He was forced to resign.

He was, however, becoming known from his published books, articles and reviews and through lecturing. He entered journalism and went freelance when he was made redundant at the beginning of the 1930s by which time he had already published *See England First* (1927), a considerable part of which is devoted to Sussex, and *Sussex* (1929) in which he claimed that in his eyes Sussex had but one drawback. "*It ruins one for everywhere else.*"

He came to the full attention of the public, becoming a household name and being christened "*Ambassador of the Countryside*", when he started broadcasting on the 'wireless' in the early 1930s. Although there were complaints about his open support for fox hunting and whisky in his talks, his broadcasts continued throughout the Second World War but did not transfer well to television when that service was restarted after the war.

He introduced people to the countryside and made it more accessible to them through his broadcasting and many of his books: not all of his some two hundred titles were on walking or the countryside. Many were and, in the 1930s, included a number that were written for and published by the railway company, Southern Railway. Amongst these was *Walking at Week-Ends* (n.d.) that describes among others a linear walk from Chichester to Cocking that passes over The Trundle: in those days rail transport was available at both ends. Mais was a constant user of public transport; he never owned a car. He strongly believed in the benefits that open air and walking could bring. On one occasion advising, in a lecture to the inmates of Lewes Prison, that they ought to get out more.

Chichester is now within sight. If Horsham at the start is sparse in major literary connections, Chichester is the opposite. So much so that there is insufficient room to include all who might be mentioned. It is possible only to skim the surface giving scarce more than a fleeting glance or a passing mention that puts little flesh on names, some of which may no longer be household and that may not now immediately excite curiosity. Chichester is a kaleidoscope: the ages, residents and visitors, abilities, genres, impressions of the city and poetry and crime. The range includes Anna Sewell (1820-78) whose father was a bank manager in the city at the time of the Crimean War. She only wrote one book but that book was *Black Beauty* (1877) published a few months before she died. She was paid £20. The book sales passed the 40 million mark in the 1990s. In addition to European languages it has been translated into Arabic, Chinese, Japanese, Hindustani and Turkish as well as Braille. It was a book that always made E V Lucas cry when he was a child. The connections come right up to date with Kate Mosse whose award winning best selling novel, *Labyrinth* (2005), gives a different and finer perspective of the Grail legend. The connections go beyond the writers. We have met a publisher and illustrators but others also contribute to getting the words on a page. Chichester has these too.

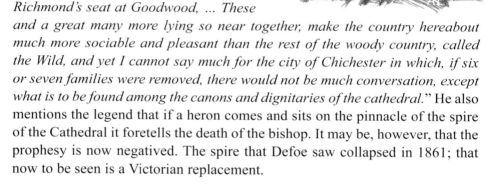

Daniel Defoe, the author of *Robinson Crusoe* (1719), was yet another prolific writer, and much else besides: soldier, spy, diplomat, journalist, being called "*the father of English journalism*", traveller and businessman, at which he failed more than once, encountering bankruptcy on the way. He did visit Chichester but he preferred the area around Goodwood. In his Tour (op cit.) he mentions that there were "*a great many fine seats of the nobility and gentlemen of the country, as the Duke of Richmond's seat at Goodwood, ... These and a great many more lying so near together, make the country hereabout much more sociable and pleasant than the rest of the woody country, called the Wild, and yet I cannot say much for the city of Chichester in which, if six or seven families were removed, there would not be much conversation, except what is to be found among the canons and dignitaries of the cathedral.*" He also mentions the legend that if a heron comes and sits on the pinnacle of the spire of the Cathedral it foretells the death of the bishop. It may be, however, that the prophesy is now negatived. The spire that Defoe saw collapsed in 1861; that now to be seen is a Victorian replacement.

Earlier, in about 1694, Celia Fiennes (1662-1741), that indefatigable traveller, mounted sidesaddle and accompanied by two maids, paused for a moment in her almost breathless pursuit across the countryside at Chichester, which she found to be "*but a little Citty encompass'd with a wall*" She notes the Market Cross: "*a very faire Cross of Stone like a Church or greate arch, its pretty large and pirramydy form with several Carvings.*" She visits the Cathedral. She climbs the tower. She looks out at the view. She gains a view down into the Cathedral from high above its floor to see "*several effigies of marble and allabaster.*" These include "*one of the Earle of Arundell and his Lady.*" And then she is off again on her travels.

Little is known of Celia Fiennes apart from what she discloses in her journal of her travels. She was born two years after the Restoration of the Monarchy under Charles II from staunch Roundhead stock. Her father, Colonel Nathaniel Fiennes, had been condemned to death for his part in the rebellion against the Crown, although later reprieved. Her three uncles and another five by marriage had all fought against the King in the Civil War. Her grandfather, the first Viscount Saye and Sele was a leading opponent of Charles I. Her journeys took her the length and breadth of England to relatives and contacts all over the country producing as she went the most comprehensive survey of contemporary England for a hundred years.

W H Hudson (1841-1922) preferred the city from a distance as, no doubt, befits a naturalist and man of the open air. He is commemorated by a bird sanctuary, and the statue *Rima* by Jacob Epstein, in London's Regent Park and, amongst whose books, *Nature in Downland* (1900) is a classic of the South Downs.

He was born near Buenos Aires in Argentina and led a vigorous outdoor life until that was ended by rheumatic fever at the age of fifteen; his interest in and observation of natural life, however, was intensified. He came to England in 1874. His writing produced little income and he lived in poverty for much of his life until he was awarded a civil pension of £150 per annum in 1901. His work is now celebrated both in Britain and Argentina.

He records in *Nature in Downland* two matters of Chichester that particularly affected him. One, an odour composed of many elements, apparently unnoticed by the inhabitants, that had a "*profoundly depressing*" effect on him. "*This depression is probably the malady commonly known as 'the chichesters', from which many persons who visit this town are said to suffer.*" The other, heralded

by many and varied signs, was the multitude of public houses and the immense quantity of liquor consumed to keep them running. There were seventy public houses with an estimated male population of 3,000 that included many churchmen and others who did not frequent them. And it was evident on the streets who had frequented them.

But it cannot all have been bad. Dr Samuel Johnson (1709-84) visited and John Keats (1795-1821) received inspiration there.

In *West Sussex Literary, Musical & Other Links* by Martin O'Neill (1996) there is reference to Dr Johnson visiting Chichester in the 1770s and the excitement caused to the local literati, one of whom pretended to be a waiter to get close to The Great Cham of Literature. He also visited in October 1782. He was staying at the fashionable seaside resort of Brighthelmstone. From there he went with his friend Mr Metcalfe, in Mr Metcalfe's carriage, to Chichester and also visited Petworth and Cowdry (sic). His comments are apparently not recorded for either occasion but there would no doubt have been a trenchant comment at anything that displeased the great man. He may have found the city pleasing, he was no countryman. The medieval city, much destroyed in the Civil War in the previous century, had given way to the Georgian that it now essentially is. He was a man of the eighteenth century age of reason before the Romantic movement expanded landscape horizons. We may not know his views on Chichester but his friend, Mrs Thrales, recorded that he detested the Downs at Brighton, "*because it was a country so truly desolate that if one had a mind to hang one's self for desperation at being obliged to live there it would be difficult to find a tree on which to fasten a rope.*"

It is appropriate that John Keats, another of the great Romantic poets, should be at the end of a literary trail that began at a memorial to Shelley. In 1819 Keats visited Chichester. He was dissatisfied with his poetry although this did not give rise to the thoughts of suicide that such occasions had provoked in him in the past. He had learnt that such feelings were a prelude to progress and that a change of scene always affected him for the better.

He came to the red brick warmth of the Georgian city and to "*old Dowager card parties.*" Mrs Lacy who was one of the hosts had rooms that included part of the medieval Vicars' Hall in the precincts of the Cathedral. These inspired the setting and feel of his poem *The Eve of St. Agnes* written in draft whilst he was in and about Chichester. The poem is based on a legend that a maiden who observes the appropriate ritual on St Agnes's Eve, 20th January, will see a vision of the man she is to marry but, in the poem, it is more than a vision. In the words of Robert Gittings, Keats's biographer who lived at East Dean, "*the poem seems like a series of medieval pictures, giving a fresh view from stanza to stanza, like some jewelled fresco from a church wall.*"

William Blake (1757-1827), poet, engraver, artist and printmaker, went to Chichester for other reasons. He lived for three years between 1800 and 1803 in the seaside village of Felpham a few miles outside the city. He had been engaged by William Hayley, of whom more later, on several designing and engraving projects but he too received inspiration from the area. The *"mountains green"* in the verse that became one of the most sung hymns, commonly known as *Jerusalem*, must be the South Downs that form a backdrop to the coastal area of West Sussex. Blake did write a poem that he called Jerusalem but that is an epic of several thousand lines. Our Jerusalem is part of the Preface to Blake's Milton of 1804.

Another long poem, although considerably shorter than Blake's Jerusalem, it contains the lines:

> *"He set me down in Felpham's vale and prepared a beautiful*
> *Cottage for me, that in three years I might write all these visions."*

Jerusalem may have become one of the most sung hymns but *The Tyger*, written before his stay in Felpham, has become the poem most anthologised in English.

But what did Blake really say to the soldier?

It started as a misunderstanding. Like many misunderstandings it escalated. So much so that it ended by Blake being tried in 1804 in the Guildhall at Chichester for assault and sedition; and this at a time when the Napoleonic War was raging and England in fear of invasion. Amongst other things it was alleged that Blake being a *"Wicked and Seditious and Evil-disposed person"* had encouraged the King's enemies to invade and had *"Unlawfully and Wickedly"* tried to *"seduce and encourage"* the King's Subjects to *"resist and oppose"* the King; Blake, it was said, had also uttered the words *"damn the King and all his Subjects."* His patron, William Hayley, paid for the defence. Blake was acquitted by the jury. The public present were according to the Sussex Advertiser *"so gratified ... that the court was, in defiance of all decency, thrown into an uproar by their noisy exultations."*

It had started the year earlier when Blake was still living in Felpham. He encountered a man in his garden. Not knowing that the man had been invited there by an assistant gardener, Blake, politely according to himself, asked him to leave. This led to a heated exchange and Blake physically ejecting the supposed intruder from the garden. The man turned out to be John Scholfield, a soldier, who may have been drinking at the Fox Inn close by. According to Blake the charges against him were made later by Scholfield and a fellow soldier as a method of revenge. The jury believed Blake; but he did have anti-monarchist sympathies.

William Hayley (1745-1820), who was born in Chichester and spent much of his life close to the city, has two claims to be part of the Literary Trail: first as a poet and biographer and, secondly, as the friend and patron of writers. Opinions are divided over his poetry. It was certainly popular. One of his volumes, *Triumphs of Temper* (1781), ran into fourteen editions and it was said that his poetry could be found on every girl's sofa. But it was hardly to critical acclaim. Dr Johnson could not get past page two: Byron said that it was, "*Forever feeble and for ever tame.*" Hayley was offered the poet laureateship in 1790. Perhaps it is not surprising that he declined.

On the other side of the coin, the visitors to his home included George Romney, the painter and Edward Gibbon, the historian. When Charlotte Smith was having no success in trying to have her poems published to pay the debts into which she had been dragged, she sent them to Hayley who agreed that she might dedicate them to him which ensured publication. He was the friend and biographer of William Cowper with whose *John Gilpin*, the "*line-draper bold*", and his adventures on horseback on an outing to Edmonton to celebrate his wedding anniversary, all from at least the older generations will be familiar from their schooldays. He was the friend and patron of William Blake, although that friendship was not always smooth. He published lives of Milton in 1804 and Romney in 1809. Maybe he is best summed up in the words of his friend Robert Southey, "*Everything about that man is good except his poetry.*"

Those who write are only too aware of the constant need for some basic reference books: help with grammar above the suggestions that are made on the computer screen that are not always helpful: a parade of alternatives are presented but where does that apostrophe actually go: and a dictionary that goes well beyond the basic computer program. Chichester had pioneers in these fields.

John Bullokar (the spelling is taken from the Dictionary of National Biography) (c1531-1609) was a grammarian and spelling reformer who came to live in Chichester and who is credited with the first book of grammar to be published in English. Little is known of his early life apart from his own writings from which it appears that he had studied civil law, had some expertise in agriculture and had seen military service abroad. By the 1550s he was a schoolmaster finding difficulties in teaching children to read and write. As now some letters had names that did not sound as the letters were pronounced, others each represented several different sounds. He embarked on a campaign for spelling reform, an aim that has been embraced by many and still lives today. He wrote a number of works but he named his grammar *William Bullokarz pamphlet for grammar or rather ... hiz abbreviation of hiz grammar for English, extracted out-of hiz grammar at-larg*. The larger grammar no longer exists but it is suspected that the title was somewhat shorter.

John's son, William, (c1574-1627) was born in Chichester. He preceded Dr Johnson both as a doctor, although William was of the medical kind, and as a lexicographer. Like his father he did not believe in brevity of titles but his *An English Expositor: Teaching the Interpretation of the Hardest Words in our Language*, published in 1616, is accepted as the second English dictionary. Although the full grandeur of lexicography was not realised until Dr Johnson's monumental accomplishment that was published nearly 150 years later.

The Bullokars were staunchly Catholic in times when penal laws prevented the open practice of Catholicism and Catholics were prohibited from public office at the risk of heavy fines and worse. The family moved from parish to parish in Chichester, possibly to avoid presentment for not attending the established church, although they did not avoid that altogether. They were also excommunicated on a number of occasions. William's son, Thomas, was ordained as a Franciscan. He was condemned to death for high treason having been arrested for celebrating mass. He was hanged, drawn and quartered in 1642 at Tyburn in London where Marble Arch now stands.

(Arthur) Eric (Rowton) Gill (1882-1940), artist, sculptor, woodcarver, letter cutter, designer, was named Eric after the hero of *Eric, or, Little by Little*.

He moved with his parents and siblings to Chichester in 1897 where he was to spend some of his formative years studying at the Chichester Technical and Art School. He left for London in 1900 to later fame and notoriety fuelled by the eroticism in his art and personal life that was at odds with his religious faith. He found Chichester "*clear and clean and rational*" and it became his model of the ideal city. He developed into an artist of genius: "*the greatest artist-craftsman of the twentieth century.*" As artist and social critic he was a writer and polemicist. He also had an influence on the practical  production of books with his designs of typefaces in the 1920s and 1930s. These included Gill Sans-serif that may be the first truly modern type face and has had a lasting impact on type design. No good computer word processing program is complete without Gill Sans amongst its fonts.

Crime has stalked the streets of Chichester. He may never have lived in Sussex but it appears from his books that J S (Joseph Smith) Fletcher (1863-1935) knew the city well. He set some of his many detective stories in the city, which he called '*Selchester*', including *The Murder in the Pallant* (1927).

Canon Victor Lorenzo Whitechurch (1868-1933), churchman, novelist, railway enthusiast and racegoer, was also responsible for some of the crime in Chichester, metaphorically that is. He was born in Chichester, studied at the Chichester Theological College and ordained at Chichester but his ministry lay out of the county. He wrote twenty four books: some detective novels with a railway background: others set in Chichester which he christened '*Frattenbury*'. His most successful novel that reached eighteen editions and sold ten thousand copies is *The Canon in Residence* (1904). It is set mainly in and around the city and the Cathedral close.

The Church's literary ambitions rose above the criminal. Locally it has known more than one poet but here it is fitting that they should be represented by Andrew Young (1885-1971). A Scot by birth and upbringing who never lost his Scottish accent, he was a Presbyterian minister at Hove. He converted to the Church of England after meeting George Bell, the renowned Bishop of Chichester, through a mutual interest in poetry that brought them together in connection with a memorial to Edward Thomas. Subsequently he was ordained and obtained a rural parish where he stayed until his retirement in 1959. He was no stranger, however, to the cloisters. He was made a canon of Chichester Cathedral in 1948. His ashes were scattered in the Cathedral grounds.

He was a leading poet with a reputation established in the 1930s. To his poetry he brought his expertise as a botanist of the first order who, it is said, had seen most, if not every British wild flower. His meticulous observation was turned to beauty on areas touched by the Literary Trail in such poems as *South Downs* and *At Amberley Wild Brooks*.

The Literary Trail ends at the statue of St Richard of Chichester, the patron saint of Sussex. This stands a short way before the main door of the Cathedral. More lies inside the Cathedral. It is hoped that the invitation of the Dean in the Postscript will be accepted to go into the Cathedral, but there is space in these pages for only three glimpses into the interior.

On the wall of the Cathedral there is a marble monument to the poet William Collins (1721-59) by John Flaxman with words by William Hayley. Collins was a true native of Chichester: born there, educated there, lived, died and is buried there although not in the Cathedral. His output was not huge and he is not now well remembered but E V Lucas called him Chichester's great poet and he was well regarded as a person by his contemporaries including the great Dr Johnson. Collins was not wholly confined to Chichester. Apart from the University at Oxford, he also spent a time in London where he was befriended by Johnson. His literary ambitions did not advance. Dr Johnson understood the problems of a man "*doubtful of his dinner, or trembling at a creditor*", and had "*delighted to converse*" with Collins and "*remember(ed) him with tenderness.*" *The Lives of the English Poets* (1779-81).

There is also a memorial to William Huskisson MP. The memorial does not mention it but his death in 1830 occurred when he became the first victim of a fatal railway accident at the opening of the Liverpool-Manchester Railway. By

one of those coincidences, Alfred Tennyson and his friend, Arthur Hallam, were passengers on the train as they returned by rather a circuitous route from Spain where they had been on a clandestine mission to take money to revolutionaries supporting constitutional government.

Finally there is the Arundel Tomb, the subject of Philip Larkin's 1956 poem of the same title: the 14th century tomb that Celia Fiennes had looked down upon from the heights of the Cathedral three hundred years ago.

... AND WHERE DO WE GO FROM HERE?

It is hoped that greater exploration has been encouraged not only of the paths of West Sussex but also of some of the writing that has a connection with it. It is customary to include a bibliography to give some guidance of where to look forward but that is not an enviable task in a work of this size where space is restricted. In the preface to his book *Sussex*, SPB Mais made no apology for adding another to the hundreds of books on Sussex. That was in 1929, nearly eighty years ago. Many more have been added since, and that is without the output of all the other writers.

Many books have what is described as a selective bibliography but, as the working bibliography for this book alone lists over seventy major sources without the many works that it was necessary to consult to verify passing references, it is needful to be highly selective. There is the natural selection imposed by the geographical limits described on page 6 that have made Kipling a notable absentee. It would also seem unnecessary to create an out of context list of the writers and their works that have been mentioned within the text. Trail guides do, however, often have lists of basic equipment starting with footwear and working upwards. The following might be regarded as such but, perhaps, for less strenuous occasions than walking the Trail.

On Sussex generally, in all its aspects, there are three marvellous books by Peter Brandon: *The South Downs* (1998), *The Kent & Sussex Weald* (2003) and *Sussex* (2006). For a look at more writers in Sussex across a wider area, there are *They Wrote About Sussex* (2003) and *Sussex in Fiction* (2003) both by Richard Knowles and *West Sussex Literary, Musical & Artistic Links* Martin O'Neill (1996). For an anthology try *Angels in the Sussex Air* selected and edited by Patrick Garland (1995).

Almost nothing has been said in this book about contemporary writing. That is part of the personal voyages of discovery to come that we hope we may have encouraged: and there are discoveries to be made both in the past and the present.

POSTSCRIPT

CHICHESTER
CATHEDRAL

I welcome those who are completing the West Sussex Literary Trail or, if you are setting out from Chichester, I wish you good luck for the journey.

Chichester Cathedral may, at first sight, seem a curious destination for a literary trail. After all, unlike Winchester, for example, no major literary figures are commemorated within the Cathedral, though of course we do have the Arundel Tomb, immortalised by Philip Larkin.

Yet Chichester as a city – small though it has always been – and the surrounding county – provide rich pickings for those with an interest in our literary heritage, as this Guide has demonstrated.

We can claim connections with Keats, Defoe, Collins, Hayley, Blake, James, Belloc, Larkin, Fry, and two significant clerical figures, Henry King and George Bell.

The Cathedral itself is, however, an appropriate place to complete the Trail, for to this place the people of Sussex, east as well as west, have brought their joys and their sorrows – the deep things of their lives – for 900 years. They have come seeking God, and in worship and contemplation have reflected on their humanity, the mystery of creation and the wonder of existence. I invite you, intrepid walkers, to do the same, and very much hope that you will enjoy your visit.

The Very Reverend Nicholas Frayling

Dean of Chichester.

ACKNOWLEDGEMENTS

Writers of fiction, which this is not supposed to be, are usually spared from having to confess that their work is other than their sole creation. For us there is the realization just how many have supported, helped and encouraged us on the way and the fear that there are those who may be unintentionally overlooked: to those our apologies.

West Sussex County Council has been with us from the start helping at many levels but our especial thanks are to Louise Goldsmith, Cabinet Member for Environment and Economy, Kim Leslie at West Sussex Record Office and the Library Service, particularly at Horsham, whose members always lived up to the Service's well deserved reputation for patience, courtesy and efficiency.

Beyond the County Council our thanks are to the Earl of Lytton, the Dean of Chichester, the West Sussex County Times and Gary Shipton its Editor in Chief, Jeremy Knight the Curator of Horsham Museum, and staff at Farlington School.

Our illustrators, Adrienne Lamb and Alison Clark, have enhanced these pages with their drawings of which they retain the copyright.

Bridget Rose, our designer has, as ever, brought peace, order and attraction to the chaos that we present her with.

We would still be a long way from the end both in words and miles without Terry Owen whom we misled into thinking he would be coming out for a quiet day's walking or two but whose input has been invaluable throughout in so many ways.

Finally there is Sally Dench who enabled us to comply with our equal opportunities policy by selflessly volunteering to carry the nails as we waymarked our way along the Trail in the early days of 2007 thus relieving the burden on those of us more challenged by the years.